Claiming the Name

A Theological and Practical

Overview

of Confirmation

Claiming the Name

A Theological and Practical

Overview

of Confirmation

John O. Gooch

Abingdon Press

Nashville

CLAIMING THE NAME:
A THEOLOGICAL AND PRACTICAL OVERVIEW OF CONFIRMATION

This book is printed on acid-free, recycled paper.

ISBN 0-687-72648-4

00 01 02 03 04 05 06 07 08 09—10 9 8 7 6 5 4 3 2 1

MANUFACTURED IN THE UNITED STATES OF AMERICA

For Nina and Carl,

*whose confirmation experiences began the thought
process that culminated in this book,*

and for Erica and Kelly,

*who were confirmed in different traditions,
and who help make our family complete.*

Table of Contents

Preface

by Herbert Lester, Jr. Ph.D.

As a pastor, I got excited about confirmation at a Jewish bat mitzvah. The event turned out to be a transforming experience and a means of grace for me.

I was a new pastor in a new appointment. The education chairperson had arranged this visit to a *bat mitzvah* for two girls as a significant part of our confirmation program, and I went along.

This bat mitzvah turned out to be a transforming experience and a means of grace for me. God used this celebration to help me develop an entirely new understanding of, and appreciation for, confirmation and its role in Christian formation.

Transforming encounters like this are very important in our faith journey. Christians are made, not born. This is why we sometimes describe our experience with God as being "born again." In Romans 12:2, Paul urged his readers: "Do not be conformed to this world, but be transformed by the renewing of your minds, so that you may discern what is the will of God—what is good and acceptable and perfect." God's transforming power meets us and shapes us in and through, and sometimes in spite of, our varied experiences.

I learned during my bat mitzvah experience that the two girls at the center of this celebration had been preparing for their confirmation all their lives. They had undergone two years of formal instruction especially for this moment. Their families and their community of faith had worked with the girls; they had expectations of them as they were being ushered into their new places in their community and in their way of life.

These girls were enlarging and maturing a covenant relationship that included

- a transmission of history, heritage, tradition, and culture from generation to generation;
- emphasis on taking one's place responsibly in the community of faith;
- the sense of continuity conveyed by this passing on of tradition;
- the embracing of the event by the community of faith;
- the use of ritual and symbols to dramatize the event.

It was all there: worship, rite of passage, character formation, family, and community. These elements have become my yardstick for formulating and evaluating confirmation ministry. They can also be found in the information, ideas, and suggestions in this book.

> **It was all there: worship, rite of passage, character formation, family, and community.**

From the very beginning of the Christian story, the concept of faith as a journey has been part of our tradition. All of us who call Jesus Christ "Lord" are on this faith journey together, regardless of our ages. Some of us are further along than others, but we are all in the process of becoming who God would have us be.

For United Methodists, this idea of faith as journey is expressed in John Wesley's image of "going on to perfection." Wesley firmly believed that we are to grow toward the time when we will know constantly and consciously the power and presence of Christ in our lives; the time when Christ will be the center point of all we think, all we do, and all we say.

On this journey, faith experiences will help shape and mold children and youth into loyal and steadfast disciples. This series of experiences begins for many in infancy, at baptism. It continues as parents, family members, Sunday school teachers, youth leaders, pastors, and other members of the congregation work to help children and youth learn and grow.

At the appropriate time, usually in early adolescence, we experience a major milestone in our pilgrimage: confirming, or making firm, our personal commitment to our baptismal faith. This act of confirming, of making our first public profession of our baptismal faith, is what we call confirmation.

Today we refer to formative ministries as spiritual formation, discipleship training, faith development, Christian education, youth ministry, religious education, or Christian religious education. No matter what we call it, however, our goal is for youth to claim the name Christian.

We want them to accept the salvation God offers them in Christ, to know how to live as Christians in our materialistic and individualistic culture, and to be able to respond to the pressures and realities of life as Christ's disciples as they continue to go on to perfection.

Confirmation is a significant step on this journey of faith.

Dr. Herbert Lester, Jr., is pastor of Centenary United Methodist Church in Memphis, Tennessee. He has served as a member of the Confirmation Task Force of the Curriculum Resources Committee of the General Board of Discipleship. He also participated in the writing/development team for the Claim the Name *resources and contributed the material on "Rites of Passage" in this book (pages 54–60).*

Beginnings

"Now the LORD said to Abram, 'Go from your country and your kindred and your father's house to the land that I will show you'" (Genesis 12:1).

The totally crazy thing is that Abram went! He didn't know where he was going; he didn't really even know the God who was calling him—but he dared to risk everything he was and everything he had for the sake of faith. Today, both Jewish and Christian traditions hold up Abram as the model for faith.

When we read the faith stories of the past in light of the chilling reality of the present, we wonder: Will our children and youth have faith? What kind of faith will they have? We live in a world that is increasingly hostile to faith, one in which people seem to get along and get ahead and do just fine, thank you very much, without any reference to God in their lives. How can we help our children and youth have faith, in that kind of world? More specifically, how can we help the young adolescents in our confirmation classes have faith?

Like Abram, each of us is on a journey of faith. Our journey has its beginnings in baptism, when we are initiated into God's mighty acts of salvation and into God's church. We grow in the faith as we are nurtured in our homes, our Sunday schools, the worship life of the faith community, and the loving care of the people of God. In early adolescence, we come to confirmation—to a significant opportunity to affirm "the faith into which we were baptized"—and make our own public profession of faith.

Whether we talk about spiritual formation, faith development, discipleship training, or Christian education, our goal is the same. We want our children and youth to know Christ, to find meaning in a relationship with Christ through the

Bible and the church. We want them to have patterns and practices of living that shape their lives and faith. And we want them to know how to make decisions that involve living out their faith. We stake a great deal of those hopes and expectations on confirmation.

> **We stake a great deal of those hopes and expectations on confirmation.**

Confirmation doesn't happen in isolation. It is not the leader plus youth, meeting in secret for a period of weeks. Confirmation is part of a process that begins with baptism and is lived out in the nurture of the family and the congregation. In fact, theologically, the congregation *is* the family. "It takes a village to raise a child"; it takes a whole church to raise a child in the faith. It is only as we are formed and transformed by God, through our participation in the life and ministry of the church, that we become Christians. Then, and only then, can we say, "I am a Christian."

But the "I" is never an isolated, individualistic ego. We become Christians only as a part of the Christian community. John Wesley was fond of saying that the New Testament has no knowledge of solitary religion. He meant that we are not "saved" in isolation. Rather, we are saved into the church, the community of faith. It is in that community that we learn the spiritual disciplines necessary for sustaining our faith and continuing our transformation into wholeness.

Through the ministry of the church, we

- learn the stories of the faith
- are empowered to participate in the ministries of God's people
- are called to commitment and challenged to ministry
- grow into the fullness of redemption

Real Christian formation—real confirmation—happens only when the community of faith is itself a conscious participant with God in God's redemptive activity.

In many ways, expecting children and youth to have faith is a radical and "countercultural" phenomenon, particularly when we insist on tying personal faith to a faith community. Spirituality and faith are everywhere in our culture; much of it is not related to a community in which that faith can be nurtured and where persons find both encouragement and accountability. To put it another way: We follow Christ out of a personal commitment, based on who we are. We do not follow Christ because society thinks that is a good thing to do.

John Wesley, like many of his predecessors in the Christian community, had a vision of Christian growth that he called "going on to perfection." His vision included the growth of the individual in love of God and love of neighbor. His vision also included the unshakable certainty that growth in love was possible only in the Christian community. He needed—and he knew that the "people called Methodists" needed—the support of others as he struggled to live out his love of God in daily life. He also needed—and he knew that the "people called Methodists" needed—the accountability for one's Christian life that could only come from being part of a community.

A "Why-to, Who-to, How-to, What-to" Book

This, then, is a "why-to, who-to, how-to, what-to" book. It is an overview of confirmation from biblical, theological, historical, liturgical, and practical perspectives. It places at our disposal the tools the church has available to assist us and our communities of faith in preparing adolescents to make their first public profession of the faith into which they were baptized. The book has four chapters:

Chapter 1: "Why?" Why do confirmation?
- an essay on "Where are we and how did we get here?"
- a theology of confirmation
- our goals for confirmation
- definitions of faith maturity
- rites of passage

Chapter 2: "Who?" With whom do we do confirmation?
- congregation
- parents
- volunteers
- mentors
- the youth
- how our understanding of youth will enrich our ministry of confirmation

Chapter 3: "How?" How do we do all that is needed for confirmation?
- Wesley's "catholic spirit" as a foundation for how we teach
- working with volunteers
- education models and how those models "pay off" in terms of teaching
- big decisions about the confirmation process
- some of the building blocks of confirmation

Chapter 4: "What?" What do we do? What resources do we have?
- ideas for involving the congregation, meeting with parents, and training mentors
- an outline of all the resources available in the Claim the Name series
- models for class sessions
- answers to frequently asked questions
- ideas for helping youth make decisions
- ideas for developing the liturgy of confirmation

A Personal Word

Work on this book really had its beginnings in the 1970's, when our daughter was confirmed. As her father and her pastor, I was concerned about the quality and depth of her confirmation experience. I struggled with the same questions when our son was confirmed four years later. In 1988, I was appointed to the Committee to Study Baptism and Related Rites, and also named the editor of confirmation resources at The United Methodist Publishing House.

Since that time, I have been immersed (or sprinkled, in the United Methodist tradition) in the theory and practice of baptism and confirmation. Long conversations with Walt Marcum, Gayle Felton, and Herbert Lester helped me clarify many of the ideas found here. Workshops; consultations; and conversations with pastors, youth workers, Christian educators, and youth themselves have helped identify questions and issues and fine-tune some answers. Ed Trimmer, Joy Moore, Gayle Felton, and Harriett Olson read the manuscript and offered many helpful suggestions. Crys Zinkiewicz, of The United Methodist Publishing House, pushed to help make this book possible. I am grateful for all their help.

John Gooch
Nashville, Tennessee, 2000

Why?

Chapter 1

Why do we do confirmation? Why do we do confirmation the way we do? Lutherans do confirmation for two or three years. Why can't we do that? Southern Baptists don't confirm at all. They just take youth into the church whenever they're "saved." Why can't we do that? To answer these and many other questions, we have to dig into our own heritage and see what we as United Methodists stand for. Only then will we be able to understand our practices and commit ourselves to excellence in those practices.

Where Are We and How Did We Get Here?

Where are United Methodists in this whole business of confirmation? On the cutting edge of a new era, where theology and practice are being reshaped.

Since 1988, United Methodists have seen a cosmic change in our theology of baptism and confirmation. First, the *Follow Me* confirmation resources helped shift the emphasis in confirmation from polity to faith, from membership to discipleship. The 1996 General Conference, in adopting "By Water and the Spirit," moved our theology of baptism and confirmation back toward our apostolic roots. We affirmed that one becomes a member of the church in baptism (at any age) and that confirmation is an affirmation of the faith into which we were baptized. Confirmation is part of a lifelong journey of faith and understanding. We are now moving even further in the direction of John Wesley and of the apostolic church by developing the idea of confirmation as a rite of sanctification.

How did we get to this point? It's a long story, because it begins with the earliest known ritual for baptism, the Church Order of Hippolytus, published sometime in the second half of the second century (A.D. 150–200). But even this order reflects a ritual that is much older.

Hippolytus lived and worked in Rome. The Christian church in Rome was as conservative a group as you would ever hope to see. The Romans disliked changes in the worship routine even more than United Methodists do! Scholars therefore think that this baptismal ritual of Hippolytus's goes back to about A.D. 100—about as close to the apostles as we are likely to get.

What do we learn from Hippolytus's order? That, in the early church, baptism and confirmation were a unified rite. The initiate was baptized, anointed with oil, received the laying on of hands (confirmation), and was admitted to the Lord's Supper—all in one service. Incidentally, this ancient rite is repeated in the United Methodist Services of the Baptismal Covenant. It is possible to anoint with oil in the sign of the cross. And the laying on of hands after the baptism (even for infants) is the same as the ancient act of confirmation.

The majority of baptisms (and, therefore, confirmations) in the early church were of adults. The church was in a missionary situation, and most of the persons baptized were, therefore, adults. However, it is also clear that whole families—including infant children—were baptized. Even the Book of Acts records instances of entire households being baptized. (The households of Lydia and of the Philippian jailer come immediately to mind.)

It is also clear that infant children of church members were baptized very early in the life of the church. Tertullian, who wrote and taught in Carthage (North Africa) from A.D. 195 to about 225, was very much an opponent of infant baptism/confirmation. Now, we all know that no one ever wastes time writing in opposition to something that does not exist. So, Tertullian's opposition tells us that, by at least 200, infant baptism seems to have been widely practiced. The writings of Tertullian and Hippolytus lead us to believe that the standard practice, even for infants, was the unified rite of baptism/confirmation.

In this act, the new Christian formally declared allegiance to Jesus Christ, and would forever after oppose evil in any form.

Why was the unified rite important? It marked the dividing line between those who were members of the community and those who were not. The renunciation of evil (Satan) was a more powerful act than the "bow" we give it today. It was a clear statement of allegiance. In this act, the new Christian formally declared allegiance to Jesus Christ and would forever after oppose evil in any form. (This is, in fact, what the statement in the Baptismal Covenant says—we just don't take it as seriously. What would it mean for us to renounce specific evils and injustices as a regular part of our participation in Services of the Baptismal Covenant?) Only after baptism/confirmation could the new member exchange the kiss of peace with the church and participate in the Eucharist. Clear dividing lines were now established between what is *included* and what is *excluded*. All the evil and injustice in the world are *excluded*. But the new Christian is now *included* fully in the life and fellowship of the Christian community.

Another element of great importance in the practice of the early church was the linkage of baptism/confirmation with a long period of nurture. Hippolytus says that, as early as the turn of the first century, the convert was taught the meaning of the faith both before and after baptism. Later, this time of nurture would cover the entire period of Lent. Candidates for baptism would meet every day with the bishop to explore the theological and ethical implications of becoming a Christian.

Prior to baptism, the emphasis apparently was on the meaning of the Lord's Prayer; a bit of the creed (the "Rule of Faith," which was much like the Apostles' Creed); and Christian rules for an ethical life. After baptism, the new Christian was led deeper into the mysteries of the faith. Some of the great treasures of our faith come from the catechetical lectures of such bishops as John Chrysostom and Cyril of Jerusalem. (If you really want to understand the faith, spend a Lent reading and reflecting on the "Catechetical Lectures" of Cyril of Jerusalem.)

The Development of Infant Baptism as the Norm

Early theologians, including Tertullian, believed that baptism restored to us the full image and likeness of God. In other words, the newly baptized Christian was in the same state of grace as Adam before the Fall. This victory theme in Christian theology trumpeted the good news that Christ had triumphed over sin and death. One of the gifts of Christ's victory was the full restoration of humanity to the image and likeness of God—to who Adam and Eve were before sin entered the world.

Tertullian went on to say that we are still responsible for the consequences of actual sin but that Christ has given us a fresh start. This "full restoration" was true for all baptized persons, including infants. (If we take Tertullian's argument to the fullest extreme, then Christians would be baptized only as they were dying so that there would be no danger of committing sin after their baptism. If that happened, they would never be full members of the Christian community; so decisions had to be made about "trade-offs.")

In the fourth century, Augustine of Hippo developed a new theology of baptism that moved the emphasis in the sacrament to infants. He argued that humanity was a "mass of damnation," born in sin because of the lust of our parents. Augustine also had major theological debates with the Pelagians, who said that babies were born good. These debates led him to some extreme positions about original sin that also affected his understanding of baptism. Only baptism, Augustine said, could save us from the awful damnation of birth sin. He wanted infants baptized as early as the age of eight days old, because they would be damned forever if they died without the benefits of baptism.

Several things are apparent here:

● If we oversimplify what Augustine said, baptism becomes magical. Just "add water" and the baby is saved.
● Here are the clear roots of all the questions about what happens to babies if they die before baptism.
● Even more important, Augustine was one of the major shapers of Western theology. We still struggle with the question of original sin and what it means for baptism.

One good thing Augustine did: He insisted that the source of the sacraments is God. Sacraments are not contingent on the moral character or beliefs of the minister, but are effective because of God. One practical result of this insistence was the repudiation of re-baptism. Even baptisms by schismatics (those who were dividing the church) was valid, because God worked through them. This has enormous implications for pastoral practice in our day, as we shall see later in this book. For now, it's back to the basic issue of confirmation.

Competing Agendas and Models in Confirmation

We have seen that, in the early church, baptism and confirmation were a single rite. During the Middle Ages, the Eastern and Western churches developed the rite in different ways.

In the Eastern Church (what we call the Orthodox communities), the emphasis has always been on the unity of initiation. Priests anoint with oil immediately after baptism, using a special oil already blessed by the bishop. A baby is baptized, sealed with the Spirit, and receives the Eucharist all at one time. This emphasis on the unity of the rite has roots deep in the tradition of the church, and has appealed to many Protestant bodies in our day.

In the Western Church, however, the emphasis fell on the connection between initiation and the authority of the bishop. Pope Innocent I summed up this attitude in 416 when he said that "clearly no one other than the bishop" is allowed to confirm. By this he meant that only the bishop could lay on hands and seal with the Spirit (anoint with oil).

So long as the "bishop" was more like what we would call a "senior pastor," this requirement was no problem. The practical flaw was the availability of the bishop. When the church spread into the great tribal dioceses of northern Europe and the bishop became an overseer and administrator more than a senior pastor, the bishop could no longer be present at every baptism to lay on hands and seal with the sign of the Spirit.

One result of this practical dilemma was the separation of what had been a unified rite, with confirmation delayed longer and longer. By the Middle Ages, years might pass before a bishop visited a community and confirmed those who had been baptized as infants. The conscientious bishops visited villages as often as possible and made the laying on of hands a meaningful moment of grace. But there are also horror stories of bishops riding through the countryside, sort of waving their arms in the general direction of baptized children lining the road, and thus confirming them.

Before we wax indignant over these past abuses, however, we need to remember how we abuse confirmation in our present practices. Busy pastors may want to "do" confirmation in four weeks. In worship, we may put more emphasis on the installation of officers than we do on confirming youth who are making an affirmation of faith. We may say that confirmation is important, but we tend to make it a low priority for our time and energy. In fact, in some churches, if adult "prospects" were given the same lack of attention given to the confirmation class, none of those adults would ever become a member.

In the early church, with the unified rite, there was an understanding that baptism/confirmation was an essential part of salvation. When, in the Middle Ages, baptism and confirmation were separated, confirmation took on a status secondary to that of baptism. In addition, baptism was increasingly seen as the salvation of an individual, without an understanding of incorporation into a community of faith.

Why, then, did the church call confirmation a sacrament? Thomas Aquinas, in the thirteenth century, was the first to admit that confirmation was "a rite in search of a theology"; he suggested that confirmation somehow "completed baptism." Some United Methodists have picked up on this statement (it has been used as an explanation of confirmation in more than one church bulletin or newsletter), although they are not clear on how baptism is incomplete. In both theology and reality, what God does in baptism is done and does not need to be "completed" or "tidied up" in some later rite.

At the Council of Trent in 1556, the question of the "right age" for confirmation first reared its head. The first answer was the age of twelve; but confirmands had to be at least seven, which was considered the "age of discretion," or the "age of accountability." All Protestant groups who kept confirmation held on to that same expectation of the "age of accountability." (Although we should note that three days after her birth, the future Elizabeth I of England was baptized and confirmed and also received the Eucharist.)

Confirmation and the Protestant Reformation

Confirmation was a problem for the Reformers. They wanted to get away from the sacramental model of the Roman church, and they could find nothing in Scripture that justified confirmation. Luther "sort of" kept confirmation, though he did not have a rite associated with it.

The key player in the Reformation was Martin Bucer, who tied confirmation to a catechetical model—examining the child on his or her knowledge of the catechism. He introduced a confirmation service that was more of an examination and graduation service than anything else. The Reformers also made confirmation a prerequisite for Communion, putting the final nail in the coffin of infant Communion and the unified rite.

What happened in the Reformation was that confirmation came to be contingent on human knowledge—in this case, memorizing the catechism. With the shift to knowledge as the key to confirmation, the sacramental side dropped out altogether. Confirmation was no longer seen as God's work, but as the work of the person being confirmed. And this in spite of the fact that the knowledge a confirmand had to absorb included a clear statement about our sole reliance on God's grace.

In another development, the Anabaptists (the historic "left wing" of the Reformation) insisted on adult baptism as the sign of a pure church. (The name *Anabaptist* means "baptize again.") For them, this meant that baptism was a deliberate choice. One had to be an adult and make a clear choice about baptism in order for the rite to be valid. Persons who had been baptized as infants could be baptized again, since their first baptism was not a valid one.

This extreme individualist position formed the roots of such contemporary statements as "I didn't have a choice about being baptized as a baby. Now I know what I'm doing, and I want to be *really* baptized." The theological danger inherent in a position like this is that the choice itself becomes a saving work totally divorced from the work of God.

Against the Anabaptists, Ulrich Zwingli, who already had a low theology of the sacraments, defended infant baptism as a sign that children were a part of the covenant community. Unfortunately, he introduced a new idea, namely that baptism was a time when parents "dedicated" their children to God. Zwingli confused confirmation with the ceremony of infant redemption in Israel. This idea of "infant dedication" continues to haunt American Protestantism. Many parents see infant baptism as a dedication, rather than baptism, and want their children baptized when they are old enough to make a personal commitment.

Later the Puritans (such as the founding fathers and mothers of the New England states) substituted a profession of faith for confirmation. This event had no sacramental overtones at all. It was simply a public profession of faith. At its best, this is the evangelical view of initiation—one has an experience of Christ that is ratified in baptism and/or confirmation. The danger in this view is that it can lead to an insistence on a datable, verifiable experience: "I was born again on Wednesday, October 3, at 3:30 in the afternoon. Here's what happened. . . ."

The strengths of the various Reform movements include

● the insistence on instruction in the basics of faith
● catechesis (being able to say what we believe)
● a personal profession of faith
● a personal ratification of the covenant

The weaknesses include

● the overemphasis on individual experience
● the weakening of the idea that baptism is the way one becomes a member of the faith community (the church)
● an emphasis on personal salvation as a "prerequisite" for baptism

The Wesleyan Heritage

John Wesley did not include confirmation in the Sunday Service he prepared for the church in America because he didn't think we needed it. Wesley's theology of baptism was that the sacrament was a unified rite and did not need to be "completed" in confirmation. It is clear, from his "Treatise on Baptism," that Wesley believed that a person became a member of the church in baptism. It is also clear that he insisted on the need for justifying grace, repentance, and conversion later in life.

But this repentance and conversion had nothing to do with "joining the church." Rather it was a part of the faith journey, a major step in "going on to perfection."

Many of the "people called Methodists" in Wesley's England were baptized members of the Church of England. So Wesley rejoiced in their new birth, but did not even consider "re-baptism" as a possible expression of their new state.

On a practical note, Wesley did always insist that the "people called Methodists" become involved in a probationary period in the class meeting. They became members of the society only after this period of shared faith and accountability. To an extent, this practice carried over to American Methodism, as well.

American Methodism struggled with the theology of initiation for nearly two hundred years, always insisting on infant baptism, but usually as a way of distinguishing us from Baptists and Disciples. The 1856 *Discipline of the Methodist Episcopal Church* said that children were to be taught the meaning of their baptism at an early age, encouraged to attend class meetings, and urged to participate in the means of grace. At an appropriate age, they were to be enrolled as probationers and then later be admitted into full membership, on the recommendation of the class leader, an affirmation of the baptismal covenant, and "the usual questions on doctrines and disciplines."

The 1864 General Conference said that the pastor shall organize classes of children ten years old or younger to teach them the meaning of baptism and "the truths of religion necessary to make them wise unto salvation"
(from the *Journal of the General Conference, 1864*; pages 202–3. Quoted in *This Gift of Water: The Practice and Theology of Baptism Among Methodists in America,* by Gayle C. Felton; Abingdon Press, 1992; page 105). By 1866, both the northern and the southern branches of American Methodism had a ritual for reception into full membership.

The 1892 *Discipline of the Methodist Episcopal Church* provided for a six-month probationary period, with teaching on the doctrines, rules, and regulations of the church. Early in the twentieth century, clergy began developing "membership classes" for children and youth. These classes were based on the idea that we need to "understand" what we are doing when we join the church.

Unfortunately, this made understanding the key to Christian experience. Interviews with United Methodist pastors as late as 1994 revealed that many of them were deeply concerned that they had to teach youth in confirmation class "everything they'd ever need to know to be a Christian" and were discouraged that they were not succeeding in this impossible task.

The word *confirmation* itself first appeared in the *Book of Discipline* in 1964. With the word came a theology of confirmation, based on a National Council of Churches document on baptism (*Baptism Confirmation . . . Implications for the Younger Generation*). It was, essentially, a three-stage process:

1. We were baptized into Christ.
2. We were confirmed in the church universal.
3. We became members of the local church.

As you can see, this was far from the unified rite of the early church. In fact, many people who bought into this theology dramatized it by stretching the ritual of confirmation out over three Sundays.

The problem was that we did not think through the implications of what we were saying, probably because of the emphasis on individualism that has so dominated our thought and practice.

> **First,** to be baptized into Christ means to be baptized into Christ's *body* (the church), as both the early church fathers and Wesley realized.

> **Second,** none of us has ever seen the "church universal." How could we be confirmed into an abstract idea? The church universal exists, in our world, only in local churches and denominations. We were needlessly repeating ourselves and confusing the people of God.

> **Third,** the emphasis on "degrees of membership" and "joining the church," as acts separate from baptism, is clearly inadequate to explain what happens in Christian initiation.

This was the situation when the General Conference adopted, in 1984, the Services of the Baptismal Covenant. Some of us working on confirmation at the general church level realized that the theology of confirmation in the new liturgy (now the official theology of the church) differed from what we had been teaching.

Then we realized that we could not have a coherent theology of confirmation without a coherent theology of baptism. This recognition led to the Committee to Study Baptism and Related Rites, and, ultimately, to the adoption of "By Water and the Spirit" by the 1996 General Conference.

Where We Are Today—A Theology of Baptism

The key conclusion of "By Water and the Spirit" is that one becomes a member of the church in baptism. We have written into our understanding of baptism the ancient understanding of the unified rite. A baptized infant of six weeks is as much a member of the church as the older adult who has occupied a pew for seventy years. One practical implication, as a side note, is that we do not bar children from the Lord's Supper.

What are the implications for confirmation?

First, confirmation is not a time when one "joins the church." "By Water and the Spirit" points to confirmation as the "profession of the faith into which we were baptized." Remember: The faith into which we were baptized is the faith of the church, summarized in the Apostles' Creed. In confirmation, a young man or woman says, I affirm the faith of the church as my own. I still don't understand it fully, but what I understand I claim as mine. This is my faith.

Second, we begin to look at confirmation as a repeatable rite. (More about this later.) If confirmation is an affirmation of faith, there may be many times in our lives when we want to reaffirm our faith in the light of new experiences and new situations. Confirmation is a process by means of which we can re-examine our faith and our life, recommit ourselves to God in Jesus Christ, and reaffirm the faith of the church in new and meaningful ways.

Finally, confirmation is a rite of sanctification. It marks those times in our life when we recognize that we have grown in faith and discipleship. Whether we affirm our faith as younger adolescents or as older adults, we mark stages in our "going on to perfection."

That's how we got to where we are. What does that all mean?

Baptism as a Sacrament

A sacrament is an act in which God does something. It is a means of grace, one of those times where, as Dwight Vogel said, "God meets us 'by previous appointment' "(*By Water and the Spirit: A Study of Baptism for United Methodists;* Cokesbury, 1993; page 9).

To say there is a sacramental view of something is to say there is an objective reality to it. Baptism is more than a sign or symbol—it is an act of God. The act of God is the objective reality. This statement lies behind much of the current debate about baptism and church membership in United Methodism. Does something actually happen in a sacrament, or is the sacrament only a sign of something that God has already done elsewhere?

Those who hold that baptism is only a sign of what God has already done have two legitimate concerns in mind. First, they are concerned about the freedom of God. Is God free to act however God chooses? Or is God's action confined to this ritual? Second, they are concerned that the sacrament not be viewed as a magical act, as if God gives grace only when we follow the correct rituals and formulas.

> **The faith into which we were baptized is the faith of the church, summarized in the Apostles' Creed.**

A part of the reality of God's freedom is that God chooses to act in certain times and places, including the means of grace. One would never suggest, for example, that prayer is only a sign of something else. We believe that God is present in prayer and responds to prayer. Surely it's not so great a leap to believe that God is present in baptism and acts through the prayers, the use of water, and the laying on of hands.

Which brings us directly to the view that something does happen in baptism. There is an objective reality. Through the sacrament, the ritual says,

> We are initiated into Christ's holy church.
> We are incorporated into God's mighty acts of salvation
> and given new birth through water and the Spirit.
> All this is God's gift, offered to us without price.
>   (from Baptismal Covenant I, in *The United Methodist Hymnal;*
>   © 1989 The United Methodist Publishing House; 33)

This is, in fact, exactly what people like Hippolytus, Tertullian, Cyprian, and a host of other early fathers and mothers believed happened in baptism/confirmation. It is what John Wesley and his first followers believed.

Baptism is, of course, not an act of magic, but a means of grace. Correct rituals are important, not because they are efficacious in themselves, but because of what they evoke in the community. In the "Thanksgiving Over the Water," we rehearse, affirm, and claim God's mighty acts in the story of faithful men and women who make up our heritage. This prayer not only invokes the presence of the Holy Spirit; it draws us again into the "mighty acts of salvation." The

Affirmation of Faith reminds us of what faith means. What we do *not* do in baptism/confirmation is affirm only our *own* faith. What a puny, second-rate, substitute that would be. What we affirm is the faith of the church, as it has been expressed for countless generations.

We say, What the church has always believed is what I believe. I lay claim to the faith heritage of my people and claim it now as my own. And part of the power of that affirmation is that *the entire community affirms the faith once again.* Affirmation is an act of the church!

So What Is Confirmation?

1. Confirmation is an act of the Holy Spirit.

In the unified rite (Baptismal Covenant I; page 37), the laying on of hands (confirmation) is accompanied by the words "The Holy Spirit work within you, that being born through water and the Spirit, you may be a faithful disciple of Jesus Christ." This is a gift of *new birth,* of prevenient and justifying grace. The Spirit, who has already given us those gifts, is now invoked to give us power to live out our baptism as faithful disciples.

What is confirmed? Is it faith? Is it the person? And who does the confirming? Is it the pastor? the congregation? the Holy Spirit? The answer seems clear: We confirm what God has already done in baptism.

> **We confirm what God has already done in baptism.**

It is certainly true that faith is involved. Even this statement raises a prior question: What is our understanding of faith? Is faith a gift? a human response to God's saving act? Is faith somehow related to doctrine? Or is the faith involved in confirmation somehow "all of the above"? Certainly, we expect that a person being confirmed will have some kind of faith in God through Jesus Christ.

We expect that the pastor and the congregation will have something of the same faith. But even faith is a gift from God. The person being confirmed is strengthened in the faith that he or she affirms. This strengthening is also God's act. So several understandings of the word *faith* are involved in confirmation.

It is certainly true that the pastor is the human agent of confirmation. It is the pastor's hands laid on the person being confirmed and the pastor who invokes the Holy Spirit. But it is not the pastor who confirms. It is the Holy Spirit, and the pastor is only the agent of the Spirit.

The congregation is also involved in confirmation, renewing its collective commitment to God and to one another and making a new commitment to the person(s) being confirmed. Parents, mentors, and others are also invited to participate in the laying on of hands. In this sense, they too are agents of the Spirit.

But pastors, family members, and the congregation also stand in need of the grace and strength promised in the rite. They are not able, in themselves, to confirm the work of God. So the full work of confirmation is the work of the Holy Spirit. Confirmation is by grace.

2. Confirmation is a means of grace.

It is God's grace that brings us to confirmation. It is God's grace that enables us to respond. Prevenient grace works through the Holy Spirit and the community of faith to cause youth to want to be confirmed. Justifying and sanctifying grace work through the time of preparation for the rite, and the rite itself, to draw the individual and the community to a new life and a new commitment.

Grace comes to the community. We are not strong enough or faithful enough as a church to stand on our own. We all stand in need of God's grace. And we stand in need *together*. John Wesley reminds us that there is nothing in the New Testament about "solitary religion," but only teachings about the church.

Together we receive God's grace through this "ordinary means" of confirmation. It is true that John Wesley excluded confirmation from the Sunday Service he sent to America. But it was a means of grace in his beloved Church of England— and it has developed as a means of grace in United Methodism in our time.

True, a personal response to grace is necessary. Both individuals and the community are called to respond to grace, to affirm their faith, to live lives of faithful discipleship. Confirmation ties together God's act in Christ (prevenient grace, salvation, new birth); the faith (and faithfulness) of the church; and the personal response of the individual into a rite that has become a means of grace.

The New Birth and Confirmation

Many United Methodist pastors have said, "We want our youth to know they have been born again." In John 3:5, Jesus says we have to be born by water and the Spirit. Being "born again" has always been an important part of evangelical Protestantism in the United States. Often, this has been associated with a specific experience of salvation. United Methodists affirm this experience. We also affirm that the new birth comes in other, less specific ways, as well.

Baptismal Covenant I says that persons who are baptized are "born through water and the Spirit." The technical theological term for this is "baptismal regeneration," a doctrine that has been around almost as long as the church itself. In the second century, Tertullian of Carthage said that we are born again in baptism into the state where Adam was before the Fall. That is, baptism literally gives us a new life. And Tertullian was sure that both infant baptism and adult baptism were the instrument of this new life.

John Wesley believed in baptismal regeneration but also in the need for continuing repentance, conversion, and acceptance of God's grace. He said in his "Treatise on Baptism" that baptism does save us, *if we live in response to it*. He also believed that we sin away the grace of our baptism (*Journal,* May 24, 1738) and that we need continually to repent, to accept God's grace, and to be reawakened in our faith commitment.

United Methodists today continue to debate the meaning and importance of baptismal regeneration. Some argue that saying we are born again in baptism turns the sacrament into a magic act, as if new birth doesn't depend on faith. Others argue that, if we depend on our faith to save us, who has enough faith to be saved? Plus, we have no trouble believing that God can choose to give new birth through the Spirit. Why do we have so much trouble believing that God can choose to give the new birth through water, that is, through the sacrament? Does God, in fact, choose to give new birth through the sacrament? The fathers of the early church thought so. John Wesley thought so. United Methodists are beginning to take baptismal regeneration more seriously in our day, even as we struggle with the full meaning of the term.

Confirmation is a rite in which we celebrate and affirm the new life God gave us in our baptism, and in other moments of growth and insight throughout our lives.

3. Confirmation in early adolescence is one of the first significant moments in which we affirm the faith into which we were baptized.

As we struggle for a coherent theology of confirmation, we find ourselves caught between the unified rite of baptism/confirmation (which may suggest that the sacrament of baptism is all we need) and the Reformation insistence on the importance of a profession of faith and on the importance of learning what the faith means. How can we reconcile the two?

In the rite of confirmation, we ask persons to renew the covenant that was made in their baptism. They are asked to affirm "the faith into which [they] were baptized." That is, they are asked to affirm the faith of the church. This is why the responsive use of the Apostles' Creed is such an important part of the ritual.

Affirming the creed is not an empty, impersonal act. If preparation for confirmation has been faithful, confirmands will be professing that they believe what the church believes. We say we believe the content of the faith as well as our own personal response to the faith.

> **Confirmation ties together God's act in Christ and our response in faith. It reminds us of the power of the community in the life of faith and promises us the presence of the Spirit on our journey.**

Always, our faith is incomplete. I used to say to my confirmation classes, "If, when we finish, you know how to ask good questions, we will have had a successful time together." Faith is always in process, and the degree to which we affirm the faith of the church changes during the various stages of our lives.

Confirmation ties together God's act in Christ (prevenient grace, salvation, triumph over sin and death, new birth) and our response in faith. It embodies the sacramental emphasis on God's action and the Reformation emphasis on profession of faith. It reminds us of the power of the community in the life of faith and promises us the presence of the Spirit on our journey.

4. Confirmation preparation and the rite itself contribute to the formation of Christian identity.

This is an incredibly important, and often ignored, point. Boys Town research on spiritual formation with high-risk youth shows that identification with a particular denomination is an important asset for youth in dealing with temptation. Being a "generic" Christian is not enough—there needs to be identity with a specific faith community.

Building identity is an important part of spiritual formation. The need for such an identity surfaces in comments such as, "My Lutheran (or Roman Catholic, or Jewish) friends know what they believe. Why don't I know what I believe?" Such questions are really pleas for identity. "Who am I? Does being a United Methodist make any difference?"

Christians in the United Methodist tradition build their faith on Wesley's "way of salvation" (original sin, justification, sanctification) and on holiness as a way of life. Confirmation preparation (done well) helps youth and adults understand the meaning of their faith and its implications for their lives. It builds in them a strong sense of identity as persons who believe and live in the Wesleyan "way of salvation."

5. Confirmation is a focus on discipleship.

The goal of confirmation (both as a rite and as an educational discipline) is to shape disciples of Jesus Christ. Church membership is one way of living as Christian disciples. Confirmation helps youth become disciples of Jesus Christ by

- recognizing, affirming, and celebrating the transforming grace of God in Jesus Christ
- responding to God's claim on their lives
- witnessing to their faith
- living into the communion of saints in its ministry to the world

All these elements relate

- to discipleship
- to accepting and affirming faith
- to making a commitment to follow Jesus Christ as Savior and Lord
- to living faithfully in the world

These last two statements relate also to vocation (as a calling) and to ministry.

Conversion and Confirmation

The New Testament words for *conversion* mean turning around or moving in a new direction. Conversion begins with God's Spirit calling to our spirits, with what United Methodists call prevenient grace. We "repent." That is, we confess that our life is not what God intended. Conversion only begins with repentance. It becomes a "turning from," and a "turning to."

We "turn away from" sin, from selfishness, from everything that oppresses us and others, from violence and evil. That's why the Services of the Baptismal Covenant begin with statements about repentance and repudiation of evil. That is the ritual in which we express our conversion.

Conversion "turns us to" faith and new life. We are converted to compassion, justice, and peace. We become citizens of Christ's new order. Another biblical meaning of *conversion* meant "a change of lords (rulers)," a new direction for our allegiance and loyalty.

Both as preparation and rite, confirmation helps us name the powers from which we turn and the evil that we commit ourselves to oppose.

Both as preparation and rite, confirmation helps us see more clearly that to which we turn. It helps us name our relationship with God, teaches us skills for building and strengthening our relationship, and supports us as we try to live out our relationship in daily life.

6. Confirmation reminds us that our vocation is to be a Christian.

All persons whom God has touched are "called" to be Christians. That is our vocation (from the Latin, *vocare*, to call). We are called to be an incarnation of the faith, as Jesus of Nazareth was an incarnation of the Word. United Methodists affirm that calling, that incarnation, in specific terms.

Our vocation is to live as Christians in the United Methodist tradition, giving flesh and blood to the "way of salvation" and the reality of holiness in the ordinary matters of daily life. The *Book of Discipline* makes that vocation clear:

> The people of God, who are the church made visible in the world, must convince the world of the reality of the gospel or leave it unconvinced. There can be no evasion or delegation of this responsibility; the church is either faithful as a witnessing and serving community, or it loses its vitality and its impact on an unbelieving world.
>
> (*The Book of Discipline, 1996,* Paragraph 107)

Our vocation is given to us in baptism. Confirmation reminds us of that vocation, which is our call to ministry.

7. Confirmation ratifies the call to ministry given in baptism.

In baptism (at any age) Christians are called to ministry. United Methodists use the phrase "the general ministry of all Christians" to express the reality of that call. Confirmation plays an important role in helping persons respond to God's call to ministry.

> Baptism is followed by nurture and the consequent awareness by the baptized of the claim to ministry in Christ placed upon their lives by the church. Such a ministry is ratified in confirmation, where the pledges of baptism are accepted and renewed for life and mission.
>
> (*The Book of Discipline, 1996*, Paragraph 106)

Those pledges of baptism include resisting evil, injustice, and oppression, and serving Christ as Lord. Certainly infants and young children are not ready to live out those commitments to any degree of fullness. Confirmation (both as rite and as preparation) ratifies the claims baptism makes upon us and provides the opportunity for a more mature commitment to ministry.

Confirmation (in adolescence) is an important moment for the ratification of our call to ministry and for beginning to live that ministry in the world. It is, however, not the last or the only moment. Throughout our lives we make new commitments to ministry in new ways. This reality of new commitments reinforces the importance of confirmation as a repeatable rite.

8. Confirmation is a rite of sanctification.

Sanctification is both gracious gift and call to life. The holy life is both a gift to be cherished and a battle to be won. Confirmation both affirms the gift and calls us to engage the struggle. In confirmation, we recognize a new level of maturity in Christian faith and life and the call for continued growth. We do not "achieve" sanctification in confirmation. But confirmation is a rite in which the confirmand affirms the gift of God's grace and accepts the call to be in ministry, indeed to be in warfare against evil and oppression.

> **Confirmation serves as an "Ebenezer," a way of marking one's passage through struggle and growth.**

Confirmation serves as an "Ebenezer" ("stone of help"; a monument erected by Samuel to commemorate a victory over the Philistines [1 Samuel 4–7]), a way of marking one's passage through struggle and growth. The "Ebenezer" significance of confirmation reminds us that sanctification is a lifelong growth in faith and love. We continue to live in and grow toward holiness of heart and life.

9. Unlike baptism, confirmation is a repeatable rite.

The Christian life does not end with confirmation in adolescence. We continue to grow in knowledge, experience, and faith. We have new experiences— college, work, military service, marriage, children, and on and on. Experiences of loss, temptation, failure, or success also help us see the need for new commitments of faith as we find our way along the journey. New experiences bring new challenges and the need for new commitment.

Young adolescents who make a faith commitment as twelve- or thirteen-year-olds are different people when they reach eleventh or twelfth grade. They have a variety of new experiences and vast new knowledge. They ask questions in different ways. Their experience of God and community has changed, and they are no longer satisfied with simple answers to faith questions.

Theologically, growth is part of God's gift of sanctification. Confirmation as a repeatable rite is an important tool in sanctification. When anyone reaches a new stage of faith and commitment in her or his life, confirmation education and rites should be offered as a way to mark that stage. Baptismal Covenant IV, the reaffirmation of baptism, was designed to provide the ritual to express the new experience and commitment to the Christian life.

This ritualizing of changed lives keeps the Reformation emphasis on struggling with faith, making honest commitments, seeking to grow in faith and understanding. It affirms the power of the Holy Spirit in life and invokes the presence of the Spirit for the next stage of the journey. It affirms the place of the congregation in nurturing and challenging lives for growth.

Confirmation as a repeatable rite frees us to rejoice in growth without raising the specter of re-baptism. The statement pastors often hear, "Now that I know what I believe and what I'm doing, I want to be *really* baptized," need not become an issue. If a person has been taught the meaning of baptism, she or he knows that God has acted in a complete way in baptism. If confirmation is understood as an act of commitment, rather than "joining the church," the person is comfortable with the possibility of celebrating the rite of confirmation again and again to indicate growth in faith and understanding.

The Holy Spirit who worked in and through the rite of confirmation also works through repeatable rites of confirmation, as Christians reaffirm their faith and make new commitments. The Spirit works in and through repeatable acts of confirmation in much the same way as the Spirit works in and through the repeatable sacrament of Holy Communion.

A congregation that is comfortable with confirmation as a repeatable rite rejoices over and over as its members witness to and celebrate the presence of God's Spirit in their lives. The ritual of baptismal renewal (Baptismal Covenant IV) is a rich resource for helping both individuals and congregations discover and celebrate times of renewal in their lives.

Confirmation as a repeatable rite opens the possibility for commitment to new forms of ministry. A young adolescent makes a willing commitment to ministry in confirmation. But that same person, as a college student or young adult, discovers the power of working for others through Habitat for Humanity or some other expression of service.

Confirmation as a repeatable rite allows for that person to witness to and celebrate new forms of ministry. It also provides the opportunity for reflection on the theological meaning of commitment.

God's House—A Wesleyan Image of Confirmation

In a little work called "The Principles of a Methodist Farther Explained," John Wesley said, "Our main doctrines, which include all the rest, are three,—that of repentance, of faith, and of holiness. The first of these we account, as it were, the porch of religion; the next, the door; the third, religion itself" (*The Works of John Wesley,* Volume VIII; Zondervan Publishing House, 1959; page 472).

Play with those images a bit. Prevenient grace leads us to the porch of God's house. Justifying grace opens the door, invites us in, and makes us a welcome member of the family. Living in the house is a gift of sanctifying grace. We have a lifetime in which to learn how to be at home in God's house and to live the kind of life to which God calls us.

Confirmation, as a rite of sanctification, marks the stage of learning to live in the house. We open ourselves more and more to God's love, to God's call to ministry, to service in God's kingdom. We enter deeper into a relationship with God. We grow in grace and love. And we return to confirmation (as a repeatable rite) to affirm and celebrate our growth, just as we return to birthdays and other special events in our earthly family.

Goals for Confirmation

Here is the basic issue: What is it we expect to happen in and through preparation for confirmation? Until we answer this question, all we can do is play around with all the other questions. Or, as the old saying goes, If you don't know where you want to go, any road will get you there. So the decision is, Where do we want to go?

Salvation and Commitment

This is the primary goal of confirmation—to help youth make commitments to become disciples of Jesus Christ. Since we are United Methodists, John Wesley becomes a good model for talking about salvation, commitment, and discipleship.

Wesley struggled mightily with his relationship with God. He wanted desperately to know that he was "saved," that God truly loved him and forgave him. John was raised in the Church of England by parents who were deeply concerned about his relationship with God. He was a graduate of Christ Church, Oxford; an ordained priest in the Church of England; spiritual director for the Holy Club; a staunch preacher of justification by faith. And *he* struggled! Is it any wonder that our youth (and indeed we ourselves) struggle with the same questions?

Recent research (The United Methodist Publishing House, 1996 and 1998) into hopes and expectations about confirmation indicates that "commitment" is a major issue. Pastors and other leaders expect that confirmation will lead to commitment to Christ, commitment to the church, and commitment to discipleship. One of the great frustrations of these leaders is that we are not able to structure confirmation in such a way that it automatically leads youth to faith in Christ.

Consider Mr. Wesley again. There were some key events in his faith struggle. One was the Holy Club at Oxford, where he and his friends tried to assure their salvation by good works. They visited prisons, gave to poor people, hired a teacher for poor children, spent long hours in devotions. They were "good Christians." But they still did not feel a sense of assurance about their relationship with Christ. Surely, if there were a structure that would lead to faith and commitment, the Holy Club was it.

A second key event for Mr. Wesley was his trip to America as a chaplain to the colony of Georgia and missionary to the Indians. A terrible storm ripped across the ship during the voyage, and John was sure he was going to die. He was terrified at the thought of facing God. In his *Journal* he wrote, "I went to America, to convert the Indians; but oh, who shall convert me?" Remember, this was a man so deeply committed to God and the church that he was willing to become a missionary to a tiny community on the edge of a howling wilderness.

A conversation about salvation was a third key event in Wesley's faith struggle. A Moravian pastor, Mr. Spangenberg, asked him, "Do you know Jesus Christ?" Wesley gave him a "correct" answer, just as we expect our confirmands to give us: "I know He is the Saviour of the world." "True," said Mr. Spangenberg, "but do you know He has saved you?" Wesley finally responded in the affirmative but later noted in his *Journal* that he was afraid he had lied.

A fourth key event was Aldersgate, where Wesley finally felt in his heart the assurance for which he had struggled so long. "I felt I did trust in Christ," he wrote, "Christ alone for salvation; and an assurance was given me that He had taken away *my* sins, even *mine*, and saved *me* from the law of sin and death." This was not so much a conversion experience (as we typically think of conversion) as it was an experience of assurance that God loved him. Note that at the time of this assurance John Wesley was thirty-five years old!

John Wesley, son of Christian parents, ordained clergy, methodical in works of piety and works of mercy, missionary to the American frontier— and he struggled with his faith!

Now, back to the question of confirmation leading youth to make a commitment to Christ. Wesley's experiences suggest several points for us to ponder.

First, there are some things we can teach and some we can't: Take, for example, Wesley's conversation with Spangenberg. We can teach our youth that Jesus Christ is the Savior of the world. We can tell them that Jesus Christ is their personal Savior. But youth have to make their own commitments to Christ and claim for themselves Christ's saving acts in history. Then they experience that which we cannot teach them—confidence in the effectiveness of God's saving grace in Jesus Christ.

Second, at Aldersgate, Wesley did not come to some powerful new insight into faith. He had been preaching justification by faith for a long time. What happened at Aldersgate is more like: "Wow! What I've been saying all along really is true! And it's true for me! Praise God!"

> ## We can help, but we can't "make it happen."

What we can do is tell youth about justification. We can tell them about God's love for them personally. We can help create settings in which youth can ponder the meaning of God's love in their own lives. We can give them all the background and understanding for experiencing that moment for themselves; we can create settings that free youth for that experience. But we cannot "make it happen."

What can we do? We can invite youth to commitment. I used to say to my confirmation classes, as we were rehearsing for the confirmation service and reviewing their questions, "Obviously, we want you to answer yes. But please understand that your yes is not a yes for all times and all possibilities. It is a yes for what you understand and feel and what you can commit to today. Next year, next week even, you'll be in a different place in your faith life. You will need to make a different commitment for where you are at that time. All your life you'll be making commitments; none of them will be final and perfect. So, at every moment, you make the commitment you can make *at that moment*."

A statement like that gives youth a sense of freedom and security. They don't have to claim something they don't have. They discover that they have room to grow in their faith and make new commitments based on that growth. One result is that they are likely to make even deeper commitments.

To use another example: Peter, early on, left his nets and followed Jesus. It was a real—and expensive—commitment. But Peter had to make his commitment over and over again. He tried to walk on the water but lost his faith. At Caesarea Philippi, he got the answer to the first question right: "You are the Christ, the son of the living God." But he failed the second half of the test and wound up being called Satan. On the last night of Jesus' life, Peter made an impossible commitment: "I will never run away and leave you." Only hours later, Peter shouted, "I told you, I don't even know him. Let me alone!"

None of this made Peter's first act of faith invalid. It simply means that his faith was incomplete when he made his first commitment. He had to struggle, and grow, and make new commitments over and over. That's a powerful lesson for us when we feel frustrated that our youth (or adults, for that matter) don't make deep commitments to Christ as a result of confirmation.

They have made a commitment that is appropriate to their age and their stage of faith development. So we also need to remind ourselves, and them, that the Christian life does not end when we are confirmed. Youth will continue to struggle with their faith; and as they grow, they will need to make new commitments over and over again.

So, we come back to the importance of seeing confirmation as a lifelong process instead of a one-time event in early adolescence. In early adolescence, youth are making commitments based on who they are and where they are in their faith journey at the moment. This is an important time for them, as they commit to making more of the journey their own. They invest in this commitment all they know of themselves, knowing that this is one stage of the journey. They will question and re-examine their faith and their commitments many times. They will need the church to stand by them in their questioning and offer them time and resources to explore their questions in community—just as Jesus did with Thomas. They will need other opportunities to affirm their faith. What happens in adolescent confirmation is only a first affirmation of faith.

A First (or Early) Affirmation of Faith

A secondary goal is to prepare youth to make their first (or an early) affirmation of faith. To set this goal in context, let's remind ourselves that the faith we affirm in confirmation is not our own faith that we have come to believe. What we affirm is *the faith of the church*. When youth affirm their faith, they are affirming what the church has believed and taught for centuries—simple statements about God the Father, God the Son, and God the Holy Spirit. Youth don't discover a new faith; they affirm the old one—and claim it for themselves.

One part of the confirmation rite is the statement, "Remember your baptism and be thankful." That statement is enough of a stumbling block for both laity and (some) clergy that we need to examine it more fully. "How can I remember my baptism?" the objection frequently goes. "I was only an infant, and I probably slept through it, anyway." This objection goes back to the theological misapprehension that baptism is somehow not valid unless the baptized is aware of the meaning of baptism and gives full consent to its administration. As we saw earlier, this stance calls into question the work of God in the sacrament. It is not nearly so important that we remember the feel of the water on our head as it is that we remember the grace of God poured out on us through the water and the laying on of hands. But, on a more practical note, how can we help people "remember" their baptisms?

"Remembering your baptism" calls for a conscious strategy that begins at baptism and continues throughout a lifetime. Here are some possible components of this strategy:

● At every infant baptism, have all the children under the age of five gather as close to the pastor as they can get. When they are teenagers, they will remember baptism vividly. The power of memory is the same whether we remember the event itself, or we remember being told about the event. This component is worth the effort, even though the congregation will need to be educated concerning its importance.

● Celebrate anniversaries of baptisms with candles, names remembered in prayer, pictures on the bulletin board. We remember birthdays in worship; what could be more important than remembering the anniversary of the new birth in Christ?

● Tell stories about baptisms in Christian education programs. Use pictures, parents or godparents, or any other memory aids to help children remember the story of their baptism.

● As a part of confirmation preparation, ask parents to tell confirmands about their youth's baptism. Encourage them to use pictures, bulletins, special gowns, or any other props that will help them tell the story. If the youth were not baptized as infants, ask their parents to tell the story about why they were not baptized.

There are many other strategies for remembering baptism, but these will help you start looking for ways to make this a conscious effort in your congregation.

Preparing for a Life of Discipleship

The other goal for confirmation is to help youth prepare for a lifetime of discipleship. Two issues are involved here, one positive, one negative.

On the negative side, confirmation has sometimes been seen as "graduation." How often have you heard a parent say, "You will stay in Sunday school until you're through with confirmation"? The implication is that, once youth have been confirmed, they no longer need Sunday school or any of the other educational ministries of the church. They have "graduated." In fact, one of the arguments for delaying confirmation until late adolescence has been that we will keep youth active in the church longer (if we "graduate" them later).

The positive issue is that we can teach youth that confirmation is only an early step in a lifelong journey. If confirmation is a first or early affirmation of the faith into which we were baptized, the implication is that they will need further affirmations. As we shall see later, adolescence is a time of questioning the faith (along with parental and other authority, our nation, and everything else in life). A multistage confirmation process, looking at confirmation as a repeatable rite, gives us a strategy for lifelong learning, commitment, and discipleship. We build on the foundation of confirmation in early adolescence, to be sure; but we continue to build.

Why not say to youth in confirmation, "This is only the first of a number of times you'll want to think about your faith and your commitment"? Lay out for them the opportunities that will be available for them in later adolescence—retreats where they will explore the faith; serious learning times in Sunday school and other settings; ways to put faith into action (work camps, service projects, missions in the community); and a structured opportunity to explore the faith in some depth prior to graduation from high school.

> **We build on the foundation of confirmation, to be sure; but we continue to build.**

This model has serious implications for the way we do Christian education with youth. If we take it seriously, we also have to take seriously the need to develop a long-range master plan for teaching youth. The master plan has to include Bible study, theology, spiritual disciplines, mission and service, and constant opportunities for raising questions about faith and life.

Several years ago, Highland Park United Methodist Church in Dallas adopted a serious, year-long confirmation program for sixth-graders, which took place during the Sunday school hour. Staff and other leaders invested huge chunks of time in developing resources for that class. The program was so successful that parents complained the next year about the quality of education for seventh-graders. The result has been a complete rethinking and restructuring of Christian education for youth in that congregation. In many ways, their youth ministry is confirmation-driven.

To build a confirmation/youth ministry that prepares youth for a life of discipleship takes a lot of work. But look at the alternatives. We can take youth through confirmation, "graduate" them, and hope they will come back to church when they have children of their own. Or we can develop a ministry that will prepare them for a life of discipleship. Given that choice, the effort involved seems more than worth it.

What About Content?

One of the persistent myths of confirmation in The United Methodist Church is that this is the time we put into the heads of young adolescents all they will ever need to know to be Christians. This notion disregards the fact that youth is a time of questioning and that "content" has to be renewed and restored on an almost weekly basis.

But what about confirmation? What do confirmands need to know? Obviously, they can't learn everything; there isn't time. And they're probably not ready for all of it. But they have to know something. What about content?

If we take seriously the multistage model for confirmation and what John Westerhoff identifies as "faith styles," we begin with the need to belong. According to Westerhoff, the faith style of younger adolescents is "belonging." One model for content is to focus on the importance of belonging in a United Methodist congregation. A part of that is to help adolescents develop the belonging skills necessary to be an active, contributing part of the congregation.

Content areas could include these topics:

- how a Christian lives (in a way that's different);
- what's unique about being a United Methodist Christian;
- practicing Christianity as a United Methodist;
- where United Methodism has come from (the history question);
- what United Methodists believe (a quick summary of United Methodist beliefs, with in-depth study coming later);
- the importance of Scripture and doctrine for understanding and experiencing our relationship with Christ;
- how to function as a professing member of the church (including skills needed in order to worship, to be part of committees, to be in ministry).

However, there is much more to learn and experience in the Christian life. Since confirmation is not the time we put into the heads of young adolescents all they will ever need to know to be Christians, we need to think in terms of a bigger picture. What that calls for is a master plan.

A master plan for Christian education for youth builds on the foundation laid in confirmation, with emphasis on

● Bible study;
● spiritual disciplines (how-tos and practices);
● experience with and reflection on mission and ministry;
● stewardship;
● the history of the church, and why that's important;
● decision-making (including refusal skills);
● a working definition of *discipleship* as a guide for faith and life;
● faith knowledge (foundational understandings, such as an exposition of the Apostles' Creed; being able to articulate one's own faith).

As part of the master plan and of a multistage approach to confirmation in late adolescence, the church can offer youth a serious look at the theological foundations of the faith. This decision also recognizes that older youth are in the "questioning" faith style, which necessarily precedes faith that is "owned," according to Westerhoff.

For years, the *Book of Discipline* has suggested that we provide youth with the opportunity to think about their faith before they graduate from high school. Paragraph 227.5 of the 1996 *Discipline* says that the content of this study should "emphasize the doctrines of The United Methodist Church and the nature and mission of the Church, leading to continued growth in the knowledge, grace, and service of our Lord Jesus Christ."

In more specific terms, the content should include, as a minimum:

● What do I believe about God?
● What do I believe about Jesus?
● What do I believe about salvation?
● What do I believe about grace?
● What do I believe about the church?
● How do I make decisions as a Christian?
● What do I believe about social justice?

Older adolescents and young adults are ready to struggle with these issues. They have raised lots of questions and are ready to tackle theology on a more serious level. *Faith Exploration for Older Youth and Young Adult*s in the Claim the Name series was written specifically to meet this need.

Our hope is that, after older youth and/or young adults have had the opportunity to explore their faith more deeply, they will also want to make a public reaffirmation of their faith, celebrating the growth and understanding that have come about as a part of their faith journey.

How Do We Help Youth Make Life-Changing Commitments?

Let's begin with another question: What does it mean to be a community of faith in a non-Christian world? Even in the United States, with a deep cultural tradition tied to Protestantism, Christianity is losing ground. Islam and the Eastern religions are increasing in numbers and influence. For many, secularism is becoming an increasingly dominant faith. The last great outbreak of spirituality led to an emphasis on individuality, rather than a strengthening of the faith community. We want our children to have faith. We are also aware of the social and cultural realities of our world. It's much easier not to be a Christian than to be a Christian.

> **It's much easier not to be a Christian than to be a Christian.**

If we take Christian faith seriously, we take a stand against the prevailing social and cultural realities. Someone once said of youth in the 13th Generation, "If you want them to be active in the church, tell them it's a way to go against their parents and the dominant culture."

That's why it is so important for us to do confirmation well. Not so we'll "get more members" for the church. Not so we'll teach seventh-graders all they'll ever need to know to be Christian. But because the choices they make are so stark and may require them to take on strong forces in the dominant culture.

So how do we help youth make commitments?

● We point out the cost of making a commitment and provide youth with stories of persons of faith who stood out against the culture of their time.

● We are honest with youth about the meaning of making a commitment. It's not just a social thing we do to make our parents or the preacher happy. It's a matter of betting our lives on God.

● We also are honest about the "benefits" of making a commitment. What happens when we commit to God in Jesus Christ? We enter into the most glorious adventure in the history of the world. And we do it in the presence of Christ.

● We provide youth with models and mentors—persons who have made a deep commitment to Jesus Christ and to the church and who live out that commitment every day of their lives.

Definitions of Faith Maturity

We not only want our children to have faith, we want them to have "mature" faith. Let's pause for a minute and consider what a mature faith might be.

The Search Institute Study

"Effective Christian Education: A National Study of Protestant Congregations" (page 10) identifies eight dimensions of a mature faith. They are

1. Trusts in God's saving grace and believes firmly in the humanity and divinity of Jesus
2. Experiences a sense of personal well-being, security, and peace
3. Integrates faith and life, seeing work, family, social relationships, and political choices as part of one's religious life
4. Seeks spiritual growth through study, reflection, prayer, and discussion with others
5. Seeks to be part of a community of believers in which people give witness to their faith and support and nourish one another
6. Holds life-affirming values, including commitment to racial and gender equality, affirmation of cultural and religious diversity, and a personal sense of responsibility for the welfare of others
7. Advocates social and global change to bring about greater social justice
8. Serves humanity, consistently and passionately, through acts of love and justice [1]

These eight dimensions can be summed up in traditional Jewish and Christian understandings of mature faith: a vertical relationship with God and a horizontal relationship with others. Jesus affirmed that the greatest commandment was to love God with all one's being and that the second was to love one's neighbor as oneself. Clearly, early adolescents will not have this kind of mature faith no matter how much information they receive and no matter how many experiences they gain in confirmation.

Mature faith is a goal of the Christian life, something toward which we continue to grow. This understanding of Christian maturity fits well with our concepts of lifelong learning/transformation and of confirmation as a repeatable rite.

[1] Reprinted with permission from Benson, Peter L., and Eklin, Carolyn H., *Effective Christian Education: A National Study of Protestant Congregations: A Summary Report on Faith, Loyalty, and Congregational Life* (Minneapolis, MN: Search Institute, 1990). All rights reserved by Search Institute, 1-800-888-7828. Search Institute, 1990.

The Mysticism of Ephesians

The Scripture also describes mature Christian faith. Look at Ephesians 4:11-16.

1. In a mature faith we recognize and claim the spiritual gifts God gives us. We use those gifts to help build up the body of Christ.
2. Maturity is measured against the "full stature of Christ" (4:13). That is, our goal is to become as much like Christ as we can.
3. Mature Christians are no longer confused by various doctrines or even "fads" in theology. They know what they believe and in whom they believe. They are able to stand firm against all the "latest things" in faith and practice. They test new ideas against the core of the faith handed down in the church.
4. Mature Christians speak the truth in love.
5. Mature Christians "grow up in every way" (4:15) into Christ. Mature Christians grow into deeper relationship with Christ. Mature Christians strive to live out Christ's love with those whom society would ignore, to live out Christ's passion for justice for the oppressed, to live out Christ's passionate hope for the coming of the kingdom of God.
6. Mature Christians recognize that they live out their maturity in the body of Christ. Each part, properly functioning, builds up the whole body—and is built up in turn.

This mystical perception of maturity is built on the image of growing into Christ. Young adolescents will not achieve this kind of maturity in confirmation classes. It will also be for them a lifelong goal and practice.

The Great Commandments

The key to Christian maturity is a life-transforming relationship with God that leads us to a life of faithfulness and holiness. It is a relationship of love with others that leads us to live a life of service and action for social justice in the world. Mark 12:28-34 is the familiar story where a scribe asks Jesus to identify the greatest commandment of all. Jesus responds:

> The first is "Hear, O Israel: the Lord our God, the Lord is one;
> you shall love the Lord your God with all your heart, and with all
> your soul, and with all your mind, and with all your strength."
> The second is this, "You shall love your neighbor as yourself."
> There is no other commandment greater than these.
>
> (Mark 12:29-31)

The implications of that statement seem clear. Both commandments came directly from Hebrew Scripture, so Jesus was relying on the faith tradition in which he had been raised. The first commandment says we are to love God with our total being, including our mind. For far too long, United Methodists have been willing to park their mind outside the door of the church, not thinking critically about either their faith or the implications of their faith for daily living. It is time, once again, to—as Wesley said—"unite the two so long divided, knowledge and vital piety."

One of the greatest favors we can do for our confirmands is to teach them critical-thinking skills. Critical thinking is not an attack on faith. Most of us know from unpleasant personal experience that we will not long hold to a faith that we cannot engage with intellectually. Nor will we ever convince the world of the power of our faith if we present it in poorly-thought-out forms.

> **The key to Christian maturity is a life-transforming relationship with God that leads us to a life of faithfulness and holiness.**

So one mark of faith maturity is the ability to think critically about our faith. If graduates of confirmation classes know how to ask the important questions, and are aware of some sources of looking for answers (Scripture, theology, faith practices, Christian community), their confirmation training and study will have been a great success.

The great biblical models for loving God and loving neighbor have always been Abraham and Sarah, the prophet Elijah, and Jesus of Nazareth. In what follows, we will look at specific episodes we can use as paradigms for living out the commandments of love.

God called Abram to leave his home, family, and everything that was familiar to him and go to a strange land. Abram wasn't even told where to go, just that God would show him when he got there. So what happened? Abram went! He just gave up everything and set out, following a call from this strange God. And, ever after, this event is held up as the great model for faith. How do we love God? We trust God completely and set out to follow God through life, even when the destination is not clear.

Is there a parallel story in Jesus' life? In Mark 14:32-42, we find Jesus praying in the garden of Gethsemane. The prayer is a familiar one: God, I know that anything is possible with you. Don't let me suffer—make the cross go away. "Yet, not what I want, but what you want" (14:36). Jesus was so committed to his relationship with God that he was willing to face death, even death on a cross, to show God's love for the world.

Abram and Jesus were both confident about their relationship with God, and their commitment to God's mission, even though they questioned it at times. To question the relationship is not a problem; in fact, questioning seems natural as the relationship grows and is challenged. The problem would be to abandon the relationship because we have questions.

Elijah was a champion of the rights of the common man, the peasant farmer in Israel who was being squeezed out of the new economic order and often defrauded of his land. The classic example is in 1 Kings 21: Naboth's vineyard. The story is simple. King Ahab wanted his vineyard; Naboth didn't want to sell it. It belonged to Naboth's family, and he had no right to give it up. Ahab was willing to abide by the law, even though it actually made him sick to do so.

Not so with Jezebel, his Phoenician queen. She had Naboth murdered in such a way that the land reverted to the state. When Ahab went to take possession, he ran into Elijah. Here's where the love for neighbor comes in. At the risk of his own life, Elijah challenged Ahab's right to take the land by fraud. He championed social justice for those who cannot fight for themselves.

One mark of Christian maturity is that we care enough about the poor, the oppressed, and those whom society shuts out that we are willing to champion their cause in the name of God—even if it costs us personally.

Biblical Models of Faith Maturity

Abraham, Sarah, and Jesus: Trusting God enough to follow

Elijah and Jesus: Caring enough to champion people society scorns

The story of Jesus driving the money changers out of the Temple (Mark 11:15-19 and parallels) echoes a similar theme. The money changers and those who sold animals for the sacrifices were providing a legitimate service for those who came to worship in the Temple. But, when someone has a monopoly on services, there is also a great temptation to take advantage of it. Apparently the money changers charged exorbitant fees to change secular coins into coins that would be accepted in the Temple. And those selling animals cut deals with the priests so that any animal anyone brought into the Temple would be deemed unacceptable. Then the pilgrims had to pay inflated prices to purchase "acceptable" animals.

The fact that Jesus overturned the tables of those who sold doves suggests that he was particularly angry at those who were taking advantage of the poor. (Doves were an acceptable offering from the very poor, who could not afford rams.) The cleansing of the Temple was a form of social and economic protest, a prophetic action on behalf of the poor. The Temple was not to be turned into a "den of robbers."

Mr. Wesley's House

Recall that in "The Principles of a Methodist Farther Explained," John Wesley wrote about the main doctrines of repentance, faith, and holiness (see page 37 in this book). For Wesley, these three elements constituted the plan of salvation.

Repentance, for Wesley, was being sorry for sin; it was also a longing for God. It is a tentative commitment, a hope that we will be accepted by God. It is not a one-time thing, but a part of our ongoing life of faith. As we come to know more and more of God, we become aware of much we need to change in our lives. Repentance is the "porch" of religion. It is not the entire religious life, but the first step toward it. When we step onto the porch, we aren't yet living in the house. Similarly, we aren't yet living the entire Christian life when we repent and turn to God. Christian maturity begins with repentance, but it does not end there.

Faith is more than just saying, "I believe." In just that much, however, it is the "door" to religion. Wesley's spiritual experience at Aldersgate reminds us that faith involves trusting that God's promises are true. It also involves the assurance that God loves us. Faith (or justification, to see the process from God's side) is like opening the door and hearing the shouts of welcome. We still aren't living in the house (the full Christian life), but we do know that we are welcome.

The aim of the Christian life, for Wesley, was holiness (or sanctification). This did not mean, for him, being morally perfect or never making a mistake. "Backsliding," after all, is an important Wesleyan doctrine. Holiness meant becoming more complete, growing into the person God intended us to become.

At one level, this sounds something like the kind of self-actualization we practice in our time. For Wesley, becoming who God intended for us to be meant growing more and more into the image and likeness of God. It was a transformation, in which God set us free from the weight of sin. It meant living so that we could say, "I live, and yet not I, but Christ lives in me." The aim of the Christian life is a life of holiness: to become like Christ.

What does Wesley's metaphor suggest to us about faith maturity and, specifically, about confirmation? Younger adolescents are focused on belonging, which is a big help to confirmation in many ways. We want youth to belong to Christ and the church. But there are two images (at least) of belonging. In one of them, youth are confirmed and become "members of the church." So they behave just like the adults—and quit coming!

Another image suggests that we move into the house and settle there, become more integrated into the life of the family, and make and live out our commitments. Wesley's metaphor allows us to say to younger adolescents, "You've only come through the front door. You're still new here, and the rooms are strange to you. You need a lifetime to live in this house, to become part of it, to explore all its possibilities."

In later adolescence, when youth are questioning their faith, the house metaphor allows us to say, "It's OK to raise questions and to explore. That's one way you learn and grow in the faith. When we move into a new house, we have to move the furniture around and hang posters in several different places before we really have things the way we want them. You're going to be testing and asking questions all your life. The church will be here to help you struggle with the questions and explore possible answers."

Being mature in the faith means that we live in the house a long time. We aren't through when we step up on the porch or even when we walk through the front door. Only after a lifetime of living does a house, or a faith, really become "ours."

How Do We Help Youth Grow in Faith Maturity?

Certain key experiences are crucial in helping youth grow in Christian maturity (discipleship). They include (but are not limited to) these ideas:

- Experiencing a community of love and accountability.
- Participating regularly in times of worship, celebration, and commitment.
- Exploring resources for Christian living "on their own."
- Developing a vocabulary to name the content of the faith.
- Knowing the stories of the faith and what those stories mean for their lives.
- Learning to think critically about themselves, their faith, and the world.

Scripture, tradition, reason, and experience are important tools for growing in faith. We are a "people of the Book," which means that Scripture always has priority as we struggle with questions of faith. We are also a specific people; so our tradition, our history (including both United Methodist history and the broader history of Christ's church through all the ages) is an important resource for faith. We use the best insights that tradition, reason, and experience have taught us as we examine the Scriptures. We interpret the Bible in the light of its own context in the ancient Near East. We interpret the Bible as a whole, and do not just lift out verses in isolation. We struggle with key questions of inspiration and authority.

Critical thinking is a key element as youth mature. We encourage our youth to raise questions and evaluate responses with the best intelligence they bring to the issue. We challenge their thinking. We encourage them to probe for deeper understanding and insight. We deal head-on with the complexities of life, rather than sliding by with "religious" answers.

Vocabulary is critically important for faith maturity. Youth (and adults) need to name what they experience so that they can talk about it. A part of that naming is to master the basics of the technical vocabulary of faith. Many people protest at this point—it's "too hard" for youth to learn all that technical stuff; and it isn't that important, anyway.

> **It's no harder to master the language of atonement and sanctification than it is to master the language of gigabytes and RAM, or corner blitz and trap blocks.**

Is it too hard? Youth learn technical vocabularies all the time. Everything they do—from science to computers to sports to music—has its own specialized vocabulary. Youth know about technical vocabularies and why it's important to use them. Recently I was talking to a boy in my class who happens to run cross country. He used a set of initials I didn't recognize, so I asked him what he meant. He defined the term and then said, "Sorry, technical term. I forgot you didn't know." My response was, "Yeah, just like technical language in talking about the faith." It's no harder to master the language of atonement and sanctification than it is to master the language of gigabytes and RAM, or corner blitz and trap blocks.

It is difficult to hold on to a faith that does not "make sense" to us. If the only language we have for expressing faith is the undeveloped language we learned in third grade, we will soon give up on the faith as being too immature. When we have a mature way to express our faith, we will delight in it and continue to grow from it.

Rites of Passage

by Herbert Lester, Jr., Ph.D.

10:45 A.M.

Sunday Morning

The worship celebration at Centenary United Methodist Church in Memphis, Tennessee, is about to start. An air of anticipation fills the sanctuary.

As the prelude winds down and the processional begins, a group of young people enters the chancel, led by their pastor. The girls wear new dresses; the boys are in shirts and ties. They will lead the worship today and give their testimonies.

Today they will make their first public profession of their baptismal faith and complete this rite of passage on their journey in Christian discipleship. Today they will be confirmed. Today is their day!

In the congregation are parents and friends, grandparents and godparents, aunts and uncles, mentors and faith-friends. In fact, the whole community of faith is gathered with the youth to celebrate this great occasion. Afterward, a reception will be held in their honor. Each youth will have a separate table on which the gathered community will place gifts to help him or her remember this marvelous day.

As Martin Marty puts it, these youth and others like them are "the center of their family's universes. They [are] going through the ordeal. They won't forget something of what the rest of us have to relearn" (from "Rites of Passage I," in *The Christian Century*, July 5–12, 1989; page 671).

Ritual is important. It can have a tremendous impact on the people who participate in it. Many of our churches have lost their power to transform lives because our post-modernism denigrates the significance of ritual, making worship no more than a sixty-minute "Thank you, Jesus, amen" session.

What Is a "Ritual"?

Simply put, a ritual is an act or a drama, either planned or improvised, that helps us leave our everyday experiences for a while and enter a different way of understanding the world. Ritual helps us create and maintain order, build community, and grow and change as individuals and as a society. For us as Christians, worship is a ritual in which we participate on a regular basis. Within these worship experiences, we celebrate rituals such as baptism and Holy Communion.

Rites of passage are particular kinds of rituals that help people move from one clearly defined status in their community to another clearly defined status. These rites are usually associated with reaching a certain level of maturity or entering a new status or profession. First documented and defined by anthropologist Arnold Van Gennep, rites can be subdivided into

- **rites of separation,** which remove persons from their former status in the community;
- **rites of transition,** which prepare persons for their new role and status in the community;
- **rites of re-incorporation,** which bring persons back into the life of the community in their new role and/or status.

Rites of passage make transitions in the community orderly and structured; they also serve several other important functions. They provide opportunities for

1. the transmission of history, heritage, tradition, and culture from one generation to another;
2. the use of ritual and symbol to dramatize the event;
3. the sense of continuity this transferring of tradition conveys;
4. the emphasis on preparation for taking one's place responsibly in the community and in the world;
5. the embracing of the event by the community.

Our society does not provide many significant rites of passage and enculturation for children and youth. In the community where the congregation I serve does ministry, the first sexual experience, the first expulsion from school, the first trip to juvenile detention, the first child, or the first incarceration as a young adult are significant rites of passage. In our church, we celebrate Sunday school promotion, getting a driver's license, and confirmation as rites of passage.

The Jewish *bar mitzvah* and *bat mitzvah* are rites of passage during which young men and women make a faith commitment similar to the one made in Christian confirmation. In the bar mitzvah and bat mitzvah, youth become "sons [or] daughters of the Law." They assume for themselves the responsibility for being faithful to God's law and living in accordance with that law. The adolescent is not, however, understood to be an adult.

I believe that confirmation can and should be a rite of passage into adolescent discipleship. Like all rites of passage, confirmation

● happens at a prescribed time in the life cycle
● involves separation and ordeal
● marks a significant change in role and status
● involves the entire community of faith

Prescribed Time

In The United Methodist Church, according to *The Book of Discipline, 1996* (Paragraph 222.3), children who are at least completing the sixth grade are recruited for confirmation. (Younger children who express a desire for confirmation education and/or preparation may be included at the pastor's discretion.) This event takes place at a prescribed time in the life cycle.

Confirmation is also a repeatable rite. People may profess the faith into which they were baptized at various times in their life cycle. The ritual of the church allows for the repeated confirming of faith on either an individual or a congregational basis (Baptismal Covenant IV, *The United Methodist Hymnal*, 50).

Separation and Ordeal

Enrollment in confirmation education can involve separation, even if only symbolically. No longer does the community of faith or the person involved see that individual as a child. No longer is that person considered a part of the church's children's ministry. Van Gennep points out that a person's voluntary willingness to participate in a ritual act, leading to a particular goal, can also be considered an act of separation. Acts of separation remove individuals from their former state or status and usher them into transition.

Once confirmands are separated from their former state, they are in a state of limbo. Neither fish nor fowl, so to speak, they have moved beyond the children's ministry but stand only at the threshold of participating-member status in the congregation. They are both "no more" and "not yet."

This transition involves ordeal; it takes some work. Youth need to be accountable, and they need to hold others accountable for their actions as well. There are no free rides in life, and confirmation is one of the best places in the world to help young people learn this lesson. Confirmation involves giving up time for classes or retreats and, sometimes, having to study during the week. The ordeal also requires moving into new areas of learning and challenge. Youth prepare to be presented to the gathered community in worship and make their first significant public profession of faith.

A Change in Role and Status

Following the confirmation experience, youth are welcomed as professing Christians in the life of the congregation. According to the *Book of Discipline,* they are now eligible to serve on task forces, committees, councils, and boards. (In some cases, youth representation is mandated.) In many churches, following confirmation, youth move from the children's to the youth ministry program.

The Community of Faith

Confirmation is not just "the pastor's job." It includes the entire community of faith. Adult leaders and mentors walk with the youth throughout the experience. The congregation supports them with prayer and affirmation. Then, during the confirmation ceremony itself, the entire community of faith recognizes this important time in the life of youth.

Because confirmation experiences are faith community events, they need to reflect the cultural and/or ethnic history and heritage of the community celebrating the event. Confirmation can be a wonderful time to commemorate and pass on that community's faith tradition, history, and heritage.

An African American Experience of Confirmation

As an African American United Methodist pastor, I want the confirmation experiences that I lead to reflect more than our shared understanding of the Christian faith and membership in the church universal. I want them to reflect the unique cultural heritage of African American people, in general, and of this congregation, in particular. I do not, however, focus attention on any understanding of rites of passage that do not emphasize equally the unique needs of both males and females. This would only foster sexism, which is as evil and destructive to our society as racism and classism.

The power of ritual should not be overlooked in creating, preparing, and administering rites of passage. People who live in a secular, urban society still have a pressing need to mark their transitions from one status to another with some form of ritualized expression.

There are no limits to the things that congregations can do in this regard. Rites of separation can involve parents and friends, the children's ministry, the youth ministry, and adults. During a special service, or at a time in a "regular" service of worship, confirmands may be ritually "separated" from their parents and from the children's ministry.

At Centenary Church, we begin our confirmation experience on Ash Wednesday with a rite of separation. Parents, guardians, and children's ministry leaders surrender confirmands to the pastor and the members of the confirmation team.

For the next year, our confirmands are in transition. During this period, adult faith friends share their faith stories, answer questions, and help the youth develop new relationships in the congregation. Mentors may also be used.

Our confirmation preparation gives continuity to the passing of tradition. We talk about what it means to be incorporated into the great story of what God has done and is doing in the world, especially in behalf of African American people. Youth also learn their local congregation's story, their family's story, and the story of their own baptism.

We also prepare the youth to accept responsible places in the community of faith and in the world. We emphasize that voting membership in the congregation, like voting membership in the larger community, assumes certain responsibilities. We tell the story of African Americans' participation in Christianity, with emphasis placed on the pursuit of excellence. In addition, the youth communicate with our lay leadership. We encourage youth to think about church leadership roles they would like to play. And we let confirmands lead their own service of confirmation.

To prepare our children to be confirmed and to be productive African American disciples of Jesus Christ, we set these pre-confirmation learning objectives:

1. Increase self-esteem and feelings of self-worth, using awareness and appreciation of African American biblical and religious history, heritage, and culture;
2. Empower youth to make nonviolent choices, and to avoid violent confrontations;

3. Memorize and understand specific passages of Scripture, the books of the Bible, affirmations of faith, and so on as preparation for making a personal profession of the faith into which they were baptized (confirmation).

Nonviolent decision-making is an important part of our curriculum. We use the "Violence Prevention Curriculum for Adolescents" developed by Dr. Deborah Prothrow-Stith, dean of the School of Public Health at Harvard, and former commissioner of health for the state of Massachusetts.

We are also intentional in our teaching methodology. We do what Thomas Groome calls "shared praxis." Traditional teaching works on a "banking" theory of education where teachers are the depositories of knowledge that they dispense to their students. Shared praxis operates on the premise that the teacher is both teacher and learner and that, by sharing the learning experience with students, all the participants grow together and are empowered as persons.

> **Confirmation is one of the high points of our liturgical year, and we pull out all the stops.**

On Easter Sunday morning, in the tradition of the early church, confirmands are re-incorporated into the life of our community of faith in their new status and role as professing members of the congregation. They are also formally received into our youth ministry.

This is one of the high points of our liturgical year, and we pull out all the stops. The event is filled with as much drama and pageantry as possible. Following the order of confirmation and reception found in *The Book of Worship,* we include laying on of hands, anointing with oil, and the Lord's Supper. At the conclusion of the service, each confirmand receives an engraved Bible as a symbol of membership in the church universal; a certificate of confirmation and church membership as a symbol of membership in this particular United Methodist congregation; and a Kente cloth stole as a symbol of membership in the African American church.

The use of ritual and symbol to dramatize the confirmation service is intended to add meaning and make the event more memorable. The use of Baptismal Covenant I, the laying on of hands, the anointing with oil, the presentation of certificates, the giving of Bibles, draping each confirmand with a Kente cloth stole, the giving of gifts, the presence of family members and friends, the community of faith—all help us accomplish our goal.

The Importance of the Community of Faith

Confirmation at Centenary has grown in almost direct proportion to

- the amount of emphasis that I, as the pastor, have placed on it
- the extent that other people in the congregation have been involved in it

A team of lay leaders works with the pastor to plan our confirmation experience. Several groups in the church plan and implement the reception following the confirmation service. The older adult fellowship gives each confirmand a personalized hymnal. Our committee on nurture and membership care, along with the parents, prepare the food for the reception. The finance committee budgets for confirmation education.

Congregational perceptions can be significantly changed by doing confirmation in this inclusive way. The youth, their families, and those people who help prepare and implement confirmation, experience a direct impact. And, in a congregation of more than three hundred active members, a project that involves thirty-five families or more is sure to make a difference.

But attitudes may be, and usually are, slow to change. As part of our ongoing Christian education program, we work to involve our congregation in theological thinking about what baptism and confirmation mean. We intentionally teach that our beliefs and practices have implications reaching far beyond ourselves.

Finally, we have come to realize that Christian education is formative; it helps shape us as disciples of Jesus Christ. Doing confirmation as a rite of passage has significantly influenced our congregational perception of confirmation and our understanding of our corporate role in it. Personally, I have been led into an entirely new understanding of the people I have been called to serve; and I have become more sensitive to aspects of the congregation's identity that I never knew existed.

This radically reorienting confirmation process at Centenary Church did not happen overnight. It took considerable effort. We had to rethink how we do spiritual formation and what we hope to accomplish in and through this ministry. To paraphrase the apostle Paul, it does not yet appear what we shall ultimately be and do in this ministry; but we pray that it will help us all grow to be like the Christ who calls us to his service.

With whom are we doing confirmation?

Silly question. We're doing confirmation with these fourteen seventh graders, all of them a lot more interested in being "cool" than in learning about the faith. And that's what's so frustrating. I really want to teach these youth the faith. How do I get them to listen?

Important question. But let's start again. With whom are we doing confirmation? There are at least five groups of people, in addition to the youth, with whom we do confirmation.

Adults Fulfilling the Baptismal Covenant

The pastor is working her way through a service of infant baptism. Everything's cool. The baby isn't crying; everyone is thinking, *What an adorable baby!* It's a good morning. Just before the congregational response, the pastor picks up the baby, walks down the aisle, and says, "This is Tim, and he is about to become the newest member of our church. In just a minute, I'm going to ask you to respond to Tim. What you will say is so important, I think you need to hear this.

"Whatever Tim needs, for the rest of his life, that will help him grow in faith, you will have already promised to give him. If he needs a Sunday school teacher, we'll say, 'Hey, it's my turn—or my gift.' If he needs a youth counselor, or someone to drive him to a youth event, or a VBS teacher, or whatever it is he needs, you will have already said that you'll do it.

"So, if you can't make that promise, if you aren't willing to give Tim whatever is in your power to give him as a brother or sister in Christ, please don't respond with the rest of the congregation."

What is this pastor talking about?

In Baptismal Covenant I, the congregation is asked, "Will you nurture one another in the Christian faith and life and include *these persons* now before you in your care?" Simply to say yes would be to commit to all the things the pastor said about the congregation and Tim's life. But look at the response the congregation makes:

> With God's help we will proclaim the good news and live according to the example of Christ. We will surround *these persons* with a community of love and forgiveness, that *they* may grow in *their* trust of God, and be found faithful in *their* service to others. We will pray for *them*, that *they* may be true disciples who walk in the way that leads to life.
>
> (*The United Methodist Hymnal*, page 35)

That is exactly what the pastor said: Whatever Tim needs, you have already promised that you will do it!

Christians have always known that it takes an entire faith community to raise a child. Raising a child in the faith is too important to be left to parents alone. And parents need the help and support of the faith community as they raise their children. So, theologically, there are all kinds of reasons the community should be involved. Let's look at some of them:

The Congregation

This is not some amorphous "blob" named "congregation." This is Tom and Jennifer and Helena and Ricardo and Ann and all the others who support youth and are role models for them. It is people who live with integrity and struggle to be faithful Christians in everything they do. It is widows in their eighties who make a regular practice of talking to youth and finding out what's going on in their lives. It is all those adults who spend their free nights for a week painting classrooms so that the children will have a clean, fresh place for Sunday school. It is the choir directors who teach songs about the faith.

Some members of the congregation have more direct roles in teaching the faith, and we will talk about them in a minute. But we will never teach the faith to children and youth without the support and the active involvement of the congregation. It is "the congregation" that makes the church and the worship service "child-friendly" and "youth-friendly."

John's Gospel tells us that, after Jesus had summoned Lazarus forth from the tomb, he turned to the people of Bethany and told them to remove the grave wrappings so Lazarus could be about his business. Jesus raised him from the dead; his family, friends, and neighbors had to set him free to live.

So?

So the congregation is to newly-confirmed youth as Lazarus' neighbors were to him. We have to set these adolescent Christians free to live as full members of the community. It's not enough to say, "We invite them to be a part of a committee, but they never come." Treat them as adults. Give them their own copy of the church newsletter (as you do with offering envelopes). Allow them to be full participants in worship.

> **The congregation is to newly-confirmed youth as Lazarus' neighbors were to him.**

Don't be like the church that asked youth to usher on the last Sunday of each month, unless the last Sunday was Communion Sunday. Then the adults took over, because Communion was important; and they had to be sure it was done right. Those youth won't be eager to do anything for the church for a long time.

Sunday School Teachers

A special group, indeed. I remember my teachers well. Mrs. Whitesell, Mrs. Cannon, Mrs. Zimman, and my mother gave hours to teaching me as a child. I learned Bible stories. I learned that church is an important and friendly place.

Churches need carefully planned programs of Christian education for children. If youth come to confirmation not knowing anything about the Bible, we need to look more carefully at what we do with children in Sunday school. Have we exposed them to the full sweep of biblical stories? What have we taught them about living in the church? about the seasons of the church year? Is there a careful plan for nurturing children in faith? Or are we just doing whatever comes along?

And the importance of Sunday school teachers doesn't stop with confirmation. Later, when we talk about faith development (pages 70–73), we will see how important it is for youth to be free to ask questions and explore what the faith really means. Youth Sunday school teachers are an important part of your confirmation team, even if they don't get the youth until after they have been confirmed.

Leadership Teams for Confirmation

As a pastor, I used to do confirmation by myself, even when I had forty-five youth in the class! What a silly mistake! I robbed both myself and the youth of a richness of faith because I elected to do the leadership on my own. If I were pastor of a church today, here's what I would do differently:

First, I would have teams of adult leaders to help plan and teach confirmation education. The planning team would work on dates, schedules, communication, worship, and celebration. They would handle logistics for field trips, retreats, and would educate the congregation on the importance of confirmation. The teaching team would take active leadership in planning and leading sessions and activities.

I would work closely with both teams and take an active role in teaching, but I would no longer be a "Lone Ranger." Youth need far more role models than just me. Plus, the team approach opens up the possibility for a wider range of teaching/learning styles and skills that allow leaders to reach more youth in more ways.

Second, I would have the planning team work with the worship work area to make the confirmation rite the focus of worship on that Sunday—and a high point for the youth and their families. The entire service would be built around confirmation. We would have banners (another sub-team) made for that class, and a reception (another sub-team) after the service.

Recruiting and building these teams (see pages 89–92 for details on how to do this) would take extra time and effort on my part; but, in the long run, it would pay off. Large numbers of key laypersons would "own" confirmation (both as rite and as education) and would be able to continue the intensity of lay involvement in confirmation after I, the pastor, left the church. In addition, these key laity would "spread the word" to the rest of the congregation about just how important confirmation is and why the congregation needs to be enthusiastically involved.

Parents

One of the largest churches in our denomination uses the parents of the confirmation class members in all the leadership roles outlined above. They plan, lead plenaries, lead small groups, handle logistics, and all the rest. One result is that these parents "own" not only confirmation, but also the entire ministry of Christian education with youth. They teach youth classes, support the ministry of education at every level, and provide crucial role models for children and youth. Many churches (and parents) may feel uncomfortable about that degree of parent involvement, but they still want parents to be closely related to confirmation. How can they do that?

A Search Institute study shows that there are two periods in early adolescence when talking with parents is crucial for faith development.

- Involve parents on planning and logistical teams to support confirmation. Even if you have some discomfort about parents in teaching roles, they will be more supportive of the whole program if they are actively involved in some constructive way.
- Have regular parent meetings to inform parents about confirmation education. Give them dates and other important information so they can plan their family needs around the confirmation schedule.
- Parents in some congregations have requested a parallel class for themselves, to study the same topics as their youth. They want to know what their youth are learning, so they can talk with them about it. In many cases, they want to know about the faith for their own sakes. They may never have learned about the faith in a systematic way, and they seize on this opportunity to cover a deficit in their own learning. A parent class will mean extra time for you and other leaders, but it will pay rich dividends in the future.
- Give parents *Claim the Name: TalkPoints for Parents and Youth* (see page 123) to help them initiate meaningful conversations with their youth about matters of faith and their confirmation experiences (something beyond the usual "What did you talk about today?" "Nothing").

The Search Institute study "Effective Christian Education: A National Study of Protestant Congregations" shows that there are two periods in early adolescence when talking with parents is crucial for faith development. One is between ages 5 and 12, when it is crucial for youth to talk with their mother about faith and God. (Only the last year or so of that period falls within early adolescence, but it is a crucial year.) The second period is ages 13 to 15, exactly in early adolescence, when it is crucial for youth to talk with mother *and* father about faith and God. Incidentally, talking with other relatives is also an important asset for youth. Family devotions and family service projects are also keys to the development of faith maturity

Most parents have almost as much trouble talking to young adolescents about faith as they do about sex. Part of the reason, in both cases, is that we know the topic is important and we're afraid we'll "blow it." But faith is so important that we have to make the effort. That's why *TalkPoints for Parents and Youth* is an important part of Claim the Name confirmation resources. *TalkPoints* won't solve all problems but it will provide some easy-to-use handles for conversation.

Mentors

The final group of adults with whom we do confirmation is mentors. (Some congregations include mature senior highs among their mentor group.) Mentors assume responsibility for youth, give them emotional support, attend classes and retreats, meet to talk with youth on a regular basis, stand with the youth during the rite of confirmation, and often remain mentors and friends for life.

Mentors function as learners and partners with youth. Mentors are not a part of the official teaching team. In every way possible, we want to communicate that mentors are co-learners. They learn from youth, as well as teach by example.

Just as parents have a Talkpoints resource, *Claim the Name: TalkPoints for Mentors and Youth* is available to facilitate building the relationship and talking about matters of faith. In today's world, with the dangers of abuse, lawsuits, and so on, you will probably want to protect both youth and mentors by having them meet in small groups. Perhaps one mentor with two or three youth, or two mentors with four to six youth. One church has Sunday lunch for mentors and youth, who eat together at the church and then do their TalkPoints. Plan to meet in public places. Incidentally, mentor-youth teams meeting at a local fast-food restaurant to talk about the faith can be an important witness to the community as well as a safety measure for all the persons involved.

I came late to the idea of mentors—in fact, after I had left the local pastorate. However, I did have one wonderful experience with mentors, quite by accident. Our congregation had "fellowship friends" for all new members. This particular year, we were celebrating one hundred years of ministry in the same building; and much of the year's program was built around the history of that church. I recruited the oldest members (in terms of years of service) to be fellowship friends for the confirmation class.

The older members instinctively took on the role of mentors. One woman was not able to get out, so the class met with her for a session. From her, we learned the roots of some of the most important traditions in the congregation. Youth also learned what UMYF was like when it was still Epworth League, why the church didn't take an offering, how they got their money, and so on. In addition, the youth learned about life and faith. The older members sent them birthday cards, bought them gifts for confirmation, and kept in touch with them for years.

It's in the Book!

No, not *that* book. This time I mean the *Book of Discipline*, the one that has all that stuff about being a United Methodist. It sets a theological foundation for the confirmation education process:

> This ministry of all Christians in Christ's name and spirit is both a gift and a task. The gift is God's unmerited grace; the task is unstinting service. Entrance into the church is acknowledged in baptism and may include persons of all ages. In this sacrament the church claims God's promise, the seal of the Spirit (Ephesians 1:13). Baptism is followed by nurture and the consequent awareness by the baptized of the claim to ministry in Christ placed upon their lives by the church. Such a ministry is ratified in confirmation, where the pledges of baptism are accepted and renewed for life and mission. Entrance into and acceptance of ministry begin in a local church, but the impulse to minister always moves one beyond the congregation toward the whole human community. God's gifts are richly diverse for a variety of services; yet all have dignity and worth.

> The people of God, who are the church made visible in the world, must convince the world of the reality of the gospel or leave it unconvinced. There can be no evasion or delegation of this responsibility; the church is either faithful as a witnessing and serving community, or it loses its vitality and its impact on an unbelieving world.
>
> (Paragraphs 106–107, the 1996 *Discipline*)

What is true for the whole world is even more true for our own children and youth. We, the people of God, either convince them of the reality of the gospel or leave them unconvinced. Often, we cannot see ways to convince the world of the truth of the gospel. We *can* see concrete, specific ways in which we can persuade our youth of the truth of the gospel. It is out of this calling that we commit ourselves to nurture in the church, the church school, and, particularly, in confirmation.

> **We, the people of God, either convince our youth of the reality of the gospel or leave them unconvinced.**

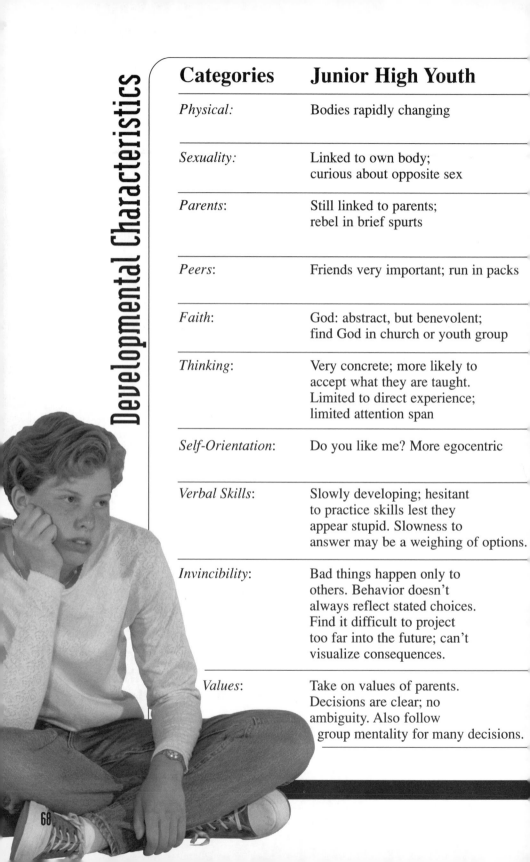

Developmental Characteristics

Categories	Junior High Youth
Physical:	Bodies rapidly changing
Sexuality:	Linked to own body; curious about opposite sex
Parents:	Still linked to parents; rebel in brief spurts
Peers:	Friends very important; run in packs
Faith:	God: abstract, but benevolent; find God in church or youth group
Thinking:	Very concrete; more likely to accept what they are taught. Limited to direct experience; limited attention span
Self-Orientation:	Do you like me? More egocentric
Verbal Skills:	Slowly developing; hesitant to practice skills lest they appear stupid. Slowness to answer may be a weighing of options.
Invincibility:	Bad things happen only to others. Behavior doesn't always reflect stated choices. Find it difficult to project too far into the future; can't visualize consequences.
Values:	Take on values of parents. Decisions are clear; no ambiguity. Also follow group mentality for many decisions.

Senior High Youth

Girls' physical changes
slowing down; boys still going through rapid change

Tied to relationships

Rebellion less intense, but
more sustained; beginning to
establish independence

Interested in longer and
more intimate relationships

Beginning of personal
relationship with God. Ask questions.

Abstract thinking; asking
deeper questions; thinking
about consequences; longer
attention span; oriented to larger world

Do I like myself in relation to others?
Move from self as center toward maturity

Most thinking done
verbally; test ideas out loud

Begin to think about
future, including career

Begin to restructure values,
but these continue to look
like the values of parents.

(Based on *Big Differences*, by Sharon Adair; Abingdon, 1998; pages 32–35)

Who Are the Youth?

One of our goals in confirmation, as in all Christian education with youth, is to help youth mature in the faith. We want them to have a strong "vertical" relationship with God in Jesus Christ, and a strong "horizontal" relationship with the church and the world. As we saw earlier (page 48), love for God and love for neighbor is as much a goal of faith development today as it was when Jesus told his disciples that these two commandments summed up all the Law and the Prophets.

To more effectively help youth move toward that goal of mature faith, we can draw on significant learnings about physical and psychological development, faith development, and learning styles. There are psychological and educational readiness factors in faith maturity, which can inform our confirmation expectations and practices.

Styles of Faith

In his important book *Will Our Children Have Faith?* John Westerhoff raised the issue of styles of faith, or ways in which the search for maturity is expressed. To oversimplify Westerhoff's thesis, he said that there are four styles of faith: Experienced, Affiliative, Questioning/Searching, and Owned. In confirmation we are immediately concerned with the first three; owned faith is an ultimate goal of confirmation but generally appears later in life.

Experienced faith is a pre-cognitive style, found most often in children (or children in the faith, of all ages). It is an experienced awareness that we are loved, that we are important to another person, that the church is a safe and fun place to be. It may even be an awareness that these adults in the church are people "I want to be like when I grow up."

Affiliative faith is the primary style of early adolescence. As the name suggests, the major issue for faith here is belonging. We want to belong, to be part of a group, to be "in." And youth will belong. They may belong to a gang, or a sports team, or a computer club, or the church. But they will belong. One obvious implication of this faith style is that early adolescence is a good time for confirmation. We "get them while they're hot," while youth want to belong to something. Our theology of baptism/confirmation says that they are already members of the church. But they need to affirm that fact of belonging in personal ways. They need to identify themselves intentionally with the church. Confirmation is an important resource to help youth with affirmation and identification.

In early adolescence, confirmation should have two major foci. One is identity. What does it mean to be a Christian? More specifically, what does it mean to be a United Methodist Christian? Who are United Methodists? What do we do or say that makes us special? What's our "inside language"? Who are our heroes and heroines? Research done by Boys Town of Nebraska on spiritual formation with high-risk youth shows that one of the strongest assets for avoiding high-risk behavior is identification with a specific denomination. Confirmation should be developing that identification.

The second focus is skills in church membership. If I'm a member of the church, how do I act? What am I expected to be? What is a steward? What does it mean to be in ministry? How do I make a contribution to the life of the church? It is important that youth know how to contribute, and in ways beyond financial contributions. Early adolescence is the time to give youth experiences of being the church in action.

Westerhoff identified two other characteristics of affiliative faith that are important for confirmation. In affiliative faith, Westerhoff says, the "religious affections" are important. It's hard for Protestants, with our emphasis on knowledge, to hear this; but the religion of the heart is crucial. For affiliative faith, the arts should be an important part of teaching and learning. Drama, music, dance, sculpture, storytelling—anything that will help create a sense of awe and mystery about the faith. I would include liturgy in the arts—the sense of holiness that comes from a powerful liturgy can enhance faith development.

The other characteristic of affiliative faith identified by Westerhoff is "authority." This doesn't mean "Do it because I said so." It does mean that the church (we're back to the importance of the congregation again) needs to "walk the talk," to live its faith story in ways that are obvious to children and youth. We act this way because of who we are.

It was said of Jesus that he spoke with authority, not like the religious leaders of his day. That authority came from Jesus' life, not just from his words. People were willing to listen to his words because they saw the way he lived. One of the great blessings that might come to youth because congregations have this sense of authority is that they would say about high-risk behaviors, "Sorry. I don't do that. I'm a United Methodist, and that's not who we are."

Experienced faith and affiliative faith are not the whole story. In later adolescence and young adulthood, youth move into what Westerhoff calls **searching faith.** Questions begin to be the focus. Youth want to know why. They argue with everything adults say. They say weird things, just to hear what they sound like out loud. If we ignore or suppress their need to go through this stage (however uncomfortable it may make us adults), youth will have "faith crises" and we will consistently lose them for the church.

During this stage is the time to teach theology. Older youth are hungry to grapple with big questions. What is God like? Do we worship one God or three? Does Jesus really save us? What does that mean? Why do we need to be in mission? Why work for social justice? What does the faith have to do with science, politics, and all the other issues we face in the real world every day?

This developmental element means that another good time for confirmation education is late adolescence/young adulthood, when we have the opportunity to respond to this searching and help youth shape a more mature faith.

Adolescents in a searching style of faith also have a need to make commitments. Their search needs to end in a commitment to someone or something larger than themselves. As Christians, we pray this commitment will be to Jesus Christ and the church. In order for youth to make that kind of commitment, we need to give opportunities for commitment again and again.

This need is one more reason why a multistage confirmation approach is so important in the life of the church. It helps us get beyond that sense of "Oh, I know I made that commitment in confirmation. But I was a little kid then. I know so much more now, and that was such a childish commitment. I need something adult now." If the church does not offer the opportunity to make more-adult commitments, youth will find some institution or person who does.

> **What is the "right" time for confirmation? Early adolescence, or late? Actually, both.**

There is a *big* difference between seventh-graders and twelfth-graders. Some of these differences are summarized in the chart on pages 68–69. We need to offer opportunities for confirmation at least twice: Once to celebrate affirmation and once to celebrate searching. Both times to allow the opportunity for making commitments and for honoring the commitments that are made. Once we get beyond linking confirmation with church membership, we can offer confirmation more than once, with each offering being uniquely tailored to the faith style of the persons involved in it.

The search is not necessarily over at the end of adolescence. Young adults (the "twenty-somethings") who don't come to worship as often as we'd like may still be in this searching mode. They too need opportunities to explore the faith, make commitments, and find a new stage of faith maturity. In addition, they need the opportunity to express that commitment in rituals of Baptismal Renewal and Affirmation. Congregations that provide opportunities for young adults to express searching faith, to explore and make commitments, and to express their faith in ritual, may discover they are suddenly blessed with lots of young adults in their midst.

According to Westerhoff, **owned faith** can emerge only after people have navigated the other styles successfully. Does our master plan for Christian nurture and education, including confirmation, provide the help needed?

Learning Styles

Youth learn in almost as many ways as there are youth, and in different ways from age level to age level (sometimes even from session to session). However, Howard Gardner and his research team identified at least seven "intelligences" (see, for instance, Gardner's *Frames of Mind: The Theory of Multiple Intelligences*; Basic Books, 1983) or ways in which people learn (see page 74 in this book). Gardner has also postulated the existence of an eighth "naturalist" intelligence, where learning takes place through interaction with the world of nature.

What do these various intelligences mean for your confirmation class? You need a wide variety of activities to engage the different "intelligences" and learning styles represented by your group. The various resources in the Claim the Name confirmation series will give you lots of options for different activities, designed to reach different intelligences.

You will tend to teach from the intelligence that is most comfortable for you personally, but don't just stay there. Stretch yourself and try some new things. Build your leadership/teaching team with persons who like to teach in different ways. For example, I teach youth regularly. I have a tendency to drift into presentation/discussion mode pretty easily. So I try to always have as my co-teacher someone who "likes games." This keeps a balance in the presentation, reaches more youth, and keeps both interest and attendance high.

With these insights into youth in general, you have greater possibilities for a more effective confirmation program. However, knowing youth in general is no substitute for knowing your particular youth. Through positive and loving relationships we make real God's love for the youth in our programs.

Ways Youth Learn

Verbal/Linguistic Intelligence
- *Definition*: uses words effectively in writing or speaking
- *Sample activities*: storytelling, word games, writing articles
- *Sample materials*: stories, word problems, creating a newspaper

Logical/Mathematical Intelligence
- *Definition*: uses numbers effectively and reasons well
- *Sample activities*: puzzle-solving, brain-teasers, writing codes
- *Sample materials*: math games, code books, debates

Visual/Spatial Intelligence
- *Definition*: determines an accurate view of the world or environment and enjoys working with it;
- *Sample activities*: map-making, art activities, imagination games;
- *Sample materials*: maps, cameras, charts.

Body/Kinesthetic Intelligence
- *Definition*: uses the whole body to express ideas or thoughts;
- *Sample activities*: mime, dance, hands-on activities, drama, roleplay;
- *Sample materials*: sports, crafts, mechanical projects, anything involving movement.

Musical/Rhythmic Intelligence
- *Definition*: sensitive to nonverbal sounds; aware of patterns in rhythm, pitch, and timbre; enjoys listening to or performing music;
- *Sample activities*: group singing; creating raps, songs that teach, songs of faith;
- *Sample materials*: hymns, creating or playing music.

Interpersonal Intelligence
- *Definition*: sensitive to feelings and moods of others; understands and interacts effectively with others;
- *Sample activities*: group discussion, outreach projects, leadership, peer teaching;
- *Sample materials*: cooperative games, discussion-starter games.

Intrapersonal Intelligence
- *Definition*: sees oneself accurately, adapts well to situations
- *Sample activities*: journal-keeping, independent studies
- *Sample materials*: computer games, self-esteem games

How?

Chapter 3

At this point the pressing question is, How do we teach? In this section, we will explore educational models for confirmation, working with volunteers, basic decisions that have to be made, some of the building blocks of confirmation, and working with a volunteer team. We begin with John Wesley.

Wesley and the Catholic Spirit

John Wesley was not particularly interested in confirmation. He believed, as a loyal member of the Church of England, that one became a member of the church in baptism. Beyond that he was concerned about justification, new birth, and sanctification. He did not include confirmation in the Sunday Service that he prepared for the Methodists in America. (Though some Wesley scholars have argued that the Sunday Service was more the work of Thomas Coke than of Wesley himself.) But Wesley's famous sermon on "catholic spirit" is helpful in terms of a foundation for teaching confirmation, just the same.

First, we need to be clear on what Wesley did *not* say in this sermon. He did *not* say that one can believe anything and still be a Methodist. This misunderstanding has led to all kinds of derisive statements about Methodists such as, "It doesn't matter what you believe, as long as you're sincere," or "Methodists are so broad-minded, they're empty-headed." This lack of definition or boundaries was not John Wesley's philosophy and it dare not be ours when we teach our confirmation classes. Even in a multiphase confirmation program, with an emphasis on belonging in early adolescence, there is still a content and a theology that we teach.

Wesley knew human nature. He knew that all people literally cannot think alike, nor can they all live their faith in the same way. So the "catholic spirit" is built on the power of love to overcome differences in faith and practice.

The text for the sermon is the story of Jehu and Jehonadab (2 Kings 10). Here were two people who were very different. Jehonadab was a strict ascetic, who practiced his faith within a narrow range of what was acceptable. Jehu was a secularist, a military leader and leader of a *coup d'etat*. He was far more interested in achieving his political ends than in a faithful religious life. What made the two men able to work together? Wesley says it was their heartfelt agreement on one essential point (ridding Israel of the worship of Baal) that led them to put aside their differences.

> **The "catholic spirit" is built on the power of love to overcome differences in faith and practice.**

Wesley said that all people believe their opinions are true; why else would they hold them? But, he said, all people also know that not *all* their opinions are true. There is an innate humility in people who think about this question at all.

One result of our awareness that not all our opinions are true is that we allow others the same freedom of thought that we want for ourselves. Another result is that we cannot force others to believe or practice as we do. As Wesley says, "God has given no right to any . . . thus to lord it over the conscience of his brethren; but every man must judge for himself, as every man must give an account of himself to God" (from "Catholic Spirit," *John Wesley's Forty-four Sermons*; London: Epworth Press, 1977; page 447).

What does this have to do with confirmation and, particularly, with educational models? It reminds us that we cannot force our own faith on adolescents, or on people of any age. What we can do is witness to our faith, try to present the faith as clearly and winsomely as possible, and hope that youth will respond to it. This means we don't teach "*the truth*." We teach the faith of the church, and invite youth to affirm it for themselves.

Wesley was also clear that the faith has a content. When he explains what he means by the heart being right, he asks questions:

● Do you believe in God? God's eternity, immensity, wisdom, power? God's justice, mercy, and truth?
● Do you believe in God's goodness and providence?

- Do you walk with faith in God?
- Do you believe in Jesus Christ, "God over all"?
- Do you know Christ crucified?
- Do you know God's justifying grace?
- Do you have assurance of your own salvation?

Those are serious questions about the content of the faith, and about one's experience of the faith. This suggests to us that confirmation education also has a content. Wesley's questions follow loosely the outline of the Apostles' Creed, or at least the first two paragraphs of that creed. This is the faith of the church, the faith that we ask youth to affirm at the time of their confirmation. As a basic educational principle, how can we ask youth to affirm that which we have never presented to them?

From belief, Wesley turns to action:

- Do you love God and neighbor?
- Do you love your enemies?
- Do you show your love by your actions?

Remember that love to God and love to neighbor are key elements of faith maturity, as we have seen it defined by the Search Institute and presented clearly in Scripture. The Great Commandment is a key definition of faith maturity. So is Micah 6:8:

> "He has told you, O mortal, what is good;
> / and what does the LORD require of you
> / but to do justice, and to love kindness,
> and to walk humbly with your God?"

Wesley addressed the practical implications of "our hearts being right with one another" under, "give me [your] hand." He again stressed that he was talking about practical love, and not matters of theology or worship. First, he said, love me as a brother in Christ. Love me patiently and kindly. Commend me to God in your prayers. Push me to love and good works. Join with me in the work of God, and let us work together.

Taking this stance does not mean giving up any of my cherished beliefs, or agreeing that whatever another person says is true. It means

Taking the Wesleyan stance of "give me [your] hand," does not mean giving up Wesleyan beliefs or agreeing with whatever someone else says is true.

opening myself in love to another, and working with that person to change the world. I can disagree with another person over the virgin birth or the authority of Scripture and still cherish that person as a friend. I can work alongside this person to overcome injustice, feed the hungry, clothe the naked, and so on.

What are the implications for confirmation education?

In addition to teaching the core content of the faith,

- we teach the value of diversity in Christ's body, the church;
- we learn to appreciate others for themselves, and, particularly, for their differences;
- we teach the importance of not judging others, always leaving judgment to God;
- we teach the importance of praying for others, particularly those with whom we disagree;
- we teach the importance of supporting those with whom we disagree in their walk of faith;
- we teach the importance of working together for God and the world—even with those who are different from ourselves.

> **Far from saying that Methodists can believe anything, Wesley's sermon on the "catholic spirit" reminds us of the importance of key elements of the faith, which all are called to believe.**

Far from saying that Methodists can believe anything, Wesley's sermon on the "catholic spirit" reminds us of the importance of key elements of the faith, which all are called to believe. It reminds us that on other matters of faith, we can live and let live. And it reminds us that we need always to live in love with others, especially those with whom we disagree.

As a model for confirmation education, it would be hard to beat those principles.

Educational Models

You may protest, "Oh, no, I really don't need a boring section on theories of education. I just want to know how to set up my confirmation class."

There is a difference between "confirmation" and "confirmation education." Educational models help us see how we do confirmation education, and how we can do it better in terms of our own goals for confirmation.

In this section, you will find

● some historic models of teaching (that you already use);
● some new trends (models) in Christian education that you will want to plug into;
● some practical ways to use those models in your own preparation and teaching.

Catechumenal Model

One of my fondest memories from seminary is that of John C. Irwin, who taught worship classes, telling about the worship life of the early church. He told us about the liturgy up to the time when they were ready to celebrate the Eucharist. Then he stood up on his toes and shouted, "Let all the catechumens depart. Let all the catechumens depart."

The catechumens were those who were preparing for church membership (baptism/confirmation). They were allowed to be present for the reading of Scripture, the prayers, and the sermon. But they were not allowed even to witness the Eucharist. They had not yet been fully initiated into the mysteries of the faith.

The educational model was simple: The catechumens met with the bishop (what we would call a senior pastor) every day during Lent (or sometimes longer) for training in the faith. The emphasis was on spiritual formation: being shaped by the Scripture, the church, the Holy Spirit. It was important to "know" something, but the "something" was more spirit-formation than information. The method was catechumenal.

The desired result was a strong commitment to Jesus Christ as Lord, and a willingness to stand against culture, in loyalty to that Lord. The educational emphasis was, What does it mean to be a Christian, and what do you need to live as a Christian?

> **The statement on baptism adopted by the 1996 General Conference reflects a catechumenal, or spiritual-formation, model of confirmation and confirmation education.**

The statement on baptism ("By Water and the Spirit") adopted by the 1996 General Conference reflects a catechumenal, or spiritual-formation, model of confirmation and confirmation education. It speaks of affirming "the faith into which we were baptized," that is, identifying and claiming the faith of the church as our own faith.

What benefits are there for you in this model? In a multistage model of confirmation, we teach younger adolescents what it means to be a United Methodist Christian, and some practical skills for living out that commitment. We teach older youth a theological, biblical basis for their faith and practice. We teach and practice spiritual disciplines. We invite youth to make commitments to Jesus as Lord at their level of commitment and understanding.

Sacramental Model

One of my senior high Sunday school class members, Kim, asked if I would do a Service of Baptismal Reaffirmation for her. (Actually, she asked if I would baptize her again; but United Methodists don't rebaptize; she and I talked our way to reaffirmation.) One Sunday morning we met at the altar during the time of commitment with the entire youth group, counselors, teachers, and family surrounding her. We "did" Baptismal Covenant IV, the service of reaffirmation, complete with the taking of vows, the use of water in ways that could not be understood as baptism, and the laying on of hands.

Kim was transformed by that moment. She had been experiencing growth in faith and understanding, and had wanted to symbolize that growth in ritual and new commitment. Today, she still talks about that moment as a new beginning for her life. That's a sacramental understanding of what confirmation (in this case, confirmation as a repeatable rite) does in the life of a person.

Here confirmation is seen as sacramental, a means of grace. The rite conveys God's grace and power to the person being confirmed. The desired result is God's transforming power in the life of the individual.

The model of education here is

- focusing the Christian education of youth on developing a relationship with God;
- being open to moments of readiness in the lives of youth so we can lead them, through the sacrament, into a sense of God's transforming power in their lives.

In practical terms, our multistage confirmation approach makes it possible for us to use this model as part of our planning for Christian education with youth. Whether we use *Claim the Name: Retreats* as an ongoing part of confirmation or engage older youth in study, using *Faith Exploration for Older Youth and Young Adults,* we open the door for God to transform lives. And we stand ready to symbolize that transformation in the rituals of the church.

Catechetical or Instructional Model

A catechetical model is based on instruction. Instruction leads to understanding and understanding leads to belief. During the Reformation, when this model first appeared, there was a specific catechism with questions and answers that persons being confirmed were supposed to memorize. The content was serious; it went far beyond memorizing the Lord's Prayer and the Apostles' Creed. There were questions about "the chief end of [humanity]," the "nature of God," and so on. The goal of this model is orthodoxy, a correct belief. The model was understanding and transfer of information; the method was often memorization. Confirmation was the period in which youth were instructed in the basics of the faith.

This model hangs on in United Methodism. Historically, we have been driven by knowledge. We have to "know something" in order to become a mature Christian, so one vision for confirmation is to teach youth all they ever need to know about the faith. When the previous official confirmation resources (*Follow Me*) were introduced, some pastors were unhappy that they did not contain enough "solid material." Some were particularly unhappy that there was no explication of the doctrine of the Trinity, since it is important that youth "understand" the Trinity. These persons were operating out of a catechetical model. Trust me on this one. I have a Ph.D. in Historical Theology. I've studied the councils that struggled with the relationship of the Father and the Son. I've even taught a graduate course on the Trinity. And I still don't understand it. Why should we expect young adolescents to "understand" what is, essentially, a mystery? Being a faithful Christian does not require an "inquiry into the home life of the Deity," as one of my professors used to say, as a prerequisite.

Please don't misunderstand. Content is important. And that content should include the basics of the faith. But we don't have to know everything in order to be a disciple. In a multistage confirmation process, we don't have to worry about "teaching everything" in early adolescence. We can teach what is appropriate for a given age level, and prepare youth (and adults) for other times of learning and growth at later stages in their lives.

One payoff for you as a teacher in using an instructional model in a multistage confirmation approach is that you can impart a lot of information. And you can enjoy teaching more, because you don't have to do it all in one shot. You can teach what is appropriate for the age and stage of the youth, knowing that you will have other opportunities to teach them more.

Profession of Faith Model

This model also came out of the Reformation, but it may have received its greatest impetus in Protestantism in the United States. The desired result is a personal profession of faith. In American Protestantism, the paradigm for profession was a personal experience that could be identified and communicated. This is partly because of the emphasis on revivalism, camp meetings, and conversion in American religious life. In one form, this model included testimony before the congregation and some kind of congregational affirmation of the validity of the conversion experience.

The emphasis is on the word *personal*. Unlike the catechumenal model, this is an affirmation of personal faith. It is "my" experience. The emphasis on personal experience is strong in many of the best-loved gospel songs: "In the Garden," "The Old Rugged Cross," and so on. The pronoun *I*, not *we*, abounds, emphasizing the individual over the community.

We all want each person to have a personal relationship with God in Jesus Christ. We want youth in confirmation to profess their faith. "By Water and the Spirit" suggests that this profession happens more than once and in different ways. In confirmation, that key document says, we affirm the faith into which we were baptized, that is, the faith of the church. Personal relationship with Christ will be touched and enriched by our confirmation experience. The relationship will grow and develop beyond the confirmation experience, as well.

> **We cannot teach for a personal encounter with Christ. Neither can we control the way the Spirit works in individual lives. We can only lay the foundation.**

We cannot teach for a personal encounter with Christ. Neither can we control the way the Spirit works in individual lives. We can only lay the foundation. We can give youth skills in spiritual disciplines and practices, help them reflect on their own lives and relationships, and prepare them for a personal encounter.

Educationally, it is also important that we not condition youth to believe their faith life is incomplete or inadequate if they do not have a specific kind of conversion experience. Instead, we need to emphasize the diversity of experiences and perspectives in the church.

The desired result in this model is a personal conversion experience, but we have to recognize that having such an experience is beyond the control of teachers and leaders. The tools used in this model include spiritual disciplines and practices and action/reflection.

Discipleship Model

What goes around, comes around. In some ways, this model goes back to the early-church catechumenal model. But it does so with a deeper understanding of human development, both educationally and in terms of faith styles. It sees faith as a journey, a process, an exploration. The model is a deliberate emphasis on discipleship, rather than membership, and on the lifelong journey of faith exploration.

The desired result in this model is a person whose journey is focused around being a faithful disciple of Jesus Christ. Faithfulness and loyalty are key components. Content is important as it helps to shape faithful discipleship.

The educational model is experiential, or action/reflection. We "do something," then think about what it means for us as Christians to have done that.

The reality of journey and process leads us to a multistage model of confirmation education. We learn church membership skills in early adolescence (a belonging style of faith) and then move to theological understandings in later adolescence and young adulthood (a questioning/searching style of faith). Both educational emphases and faith styles are appropriate for different stages in the journey of faith.

Sanctification Model

"Are you going on to perfection?" "Do you expect to be made perfect in love in this life?" All United Methodist clergy had to answer those questions when they became members of an annual conference. But here's the "kicker"—Wesley intended that *all* the "people called Methodist" strive after perfection.

This is not the place for a detailed discussion of sanctification, but let's remind ourselves that it is 1) always a gift of God's grace, and 2) always a goal of the Christian life. Further, sanctification has to do with love for God and neighbor (that is, with faith maturity) and not with freedom from errors or mistakes in all areas of our lives.

As a model for confirmation, sanctification builds on the discipleship, or developmental, model. In many ways, it is the next stage in discipleship. The desired result is a disciple. Here the goal of discipleship is perfect love, a fullness of faith that only God can give.

In the early centuries of the church, thousands of men and women heard Jesus' words to the young man, "You lack one thing; go, sell what you own, and give the money to the poor, and you will have treasure in heaven; then come, follow me" (Mark 10:21). They obeyed those words literally, and fueled the great move toward monasticism in the church. This was the expression of their commitment to perfection. John Wesley called his followers to seek personal perfection *in* the world, rather than in seclusion *from* the world. In other words, what does it mean to be a Christian in a world of clashing economic expectations, consumerism, school shootings, and substance abuse?

The desired result of this model is a mature Christian. Maturity is a lifelong process, so our educational model is really "continuing education."

Confirmation in early adolescence is only an early stage in the journey. Confirmation as a repeatable rite allows us to engage in continuing education for youth and adults, helping them grow in faith, understanding, practice, and challenge. Usually we discover that about the time we think we're doing OK, God says to us, "Now here's this other thing you need to work on."

A sanctification model helps us understand and live in response to God's work in our lives. It emphasizes the need for continual growth in our faith and practice. It leads us to change practices in an attempt to follow Jesus' teaching. And it opens the door for continuing education for all Christians.

> **A sanctification model helps us understand and live in response to God's work in our lives. It emphasizes the need for continual growth in our faith and practice.**

The continuing education model builds on affiliation and affirmation. It responds to and struggles with questions and searching. It encourages people to explore new horizons of faith and practice. It teaches spiritual disciplines, and helps people discover and use the gifts the Spirit has given them.

Some Contemporary Trends

Robert L. Browning and Roy A. Reed, in *Models of Confirmation and Baptismal Affirmation* (Religious Education Press, 1995), identified what they call major trends in religious education that affect confirmation education (pages 39–50). Briefly, those trends are these:

1. **The movement from religious education for assent to right beliefs to a religious education that interrelates beliefs and a quest for truth that can be integrated with all of life.**

To oversimplify, this is the movement from catechism to discipleship/ sanctification outlined above. The key to this trend is teaching doctrine so that people know the traditions of their denomination and where they are in relationship to its values and identity. The key questions are always, "Why? Why should I believe that? What is important about that teaching? Why should I commit to that position?"

2. **The movement from a theory-to-practice approach to a shared praxis approach in which theory and practice are in ongoing interaction.**

"Theory to practice" is another way of saying "Bible to life" or "doctrine to life." The paradigm for this movement was the shared curriculum plan developed by sixteen denominations in the 1950's and 60's. For confirmation, it moved toward relating the gospel to life concerns of youth. The new way is clearly seen in Thomas Groome's "shared praxis" model. It is a five-step approach that ties life and faith closely together, naming the faith in response to issues raised by the stories and issues of participants. In a way, this is a "life-to-Bible" model, but it is also more than that. It is an action-reflection-action model.

3. **The movement beyond a nurture model of religious education to a faith development perspective.**

James Fowler and John Westerhoff are two prominent examples of this faith development perspective. As we have already seen in this book, faith development leads us to adapt confirmation education to the faith stage/style of the learners and to offer a multistage approach to confirmation as a way of helping people continue to develop and grow in faith.

4. **The movement away from schooling as the primary strategy for Christian education toward a congregational or community of faith approach inside of which schooling in various forms will still have an important place.**

Until recently, confirmation followed a schooling model, with classes, homework, field trips, and so on. The community of faith model puts a stronger emphasis on participation in the faith community as a learning strategy. Charles Foster, John Westerhoff, and William Willimon have all made major contributions to this model. For confirmation, one of the key strategies to arise from this model is the use of mentors. Another is the use of leadership teams for confirmation education.

5. **The movement from a split between liturgy and religious education to an approach that brings liturgy and religious education together as partners.**

This new model means a reflection on liturgy, particularly the liturgical calendar, as a key strategy in religious education. One element in *Claim the Name: Confirmation Teaching Plans for 6–15 Weeks* is the use of the Christian Year. The advantage of this approach is that every year as the seasons change, the youth will have the teachings of their confirmation classes reinforced.

6. A movement toward the integration of religious education and spirituality.

Spirituality, defined as "a celebration of God's ongoing creation in each of our lives, as an affirmation of the whole person" (from *Models of Confirmation and Baptismal Affirmation*; page 49), is a call to responsibility before God in the world. Ways of integrating spirituality include imagination, reflection on Scripture, meditation, prayer, writing in journals, becoming aware of God's presence in the group itself.

So what do we do with all these models? Most leaders of confirmation programs have, either consciously or unconsciously, a model and method they follow. Exploring other models and methods may help us see other ways in which we could enrich what we do and help youth grow in faith.

> **Consider the benefits of other models and methods. When you know what your goal for confirmation education is, you can select the best from many models.**

Probably no one follows a single model exclusively. A non-scientific survey of confirmation leaders from local churches showed that most of the people surveyed used elements of three or more of these models. So, choose what works for you. Consider the benefits of other models and methods. When you know what your goal for confirmation education is, you can select the best from many models and still be true to your own process.

Working With Volunteers

Why can't I just lead the confirmation class by myself and not mess with all the extra effort of recruiting and training volunteers? Well, you can, of course. That's what I did for years. Let me tell you what I think I missed in all that.

● First, I missed some wonderful relationships with talented, caring adults.
● Second, because I was "too busy" to spend time recruiting and training helpers, I spent a lot of energy and time in the actual teaching that, if shared, would have been more effective. (*Axiom: Energy spent up front is paid back two or three times later in the confirmation process.*)

- Third, I missed giving youth the opportunity to relate with many adults who cared about them and about the faith. Which means I also missed an opportunity to build up the body of Christ, because I did not allow laity to participate fully in the ministry of teaching.
- Finally, I also missed a chance for the congregation to learn through the confirmation process.

What would I do differently if I were back in the parish today?

Before, I always began confirmation classes in January and went through Pentecost. And, I did it alone. Here's what I would do differently:

- I would begin to recruit my volunteer teams in July;
- We would begin meeting together in late September or early October (see pages 90–92 for what we would do in those meetings);
- In January, we would begin teaching the confirmation class as a team. I would be a part of the team, and not the "expert" or the "head honcho." (That would take serious effort on my part, because teaching is one of my spiritual gifts and I love to do it; I would have to work hard to keep "hands off" when other team members were leading.)

The Benefits of a Leadership Team

- Youth have more than one model for the faith journey, and more than one adult with whom they can talk;
- Adults grow in their own faith and discipleship as they work with confirmands;
- Adults provide a built-in protection for youth and other adults, and help call all persons to accountability in the process;
- Youth and adults build a community of faith, which becomes a model for the community of faith in the congregation;
- Adults bring to the conversation a broad range of experience with life and a wide variety of faith stories. This richness of experience adds depth and meaning to the faith journey through confirmation—and life. Using partners also models confirmation as the work of the whole congregation, not just an assignment given to pastors, youth ministers, or Christian educators.

Recruiting and Training Volunteers

Whom do we recruit?

There are several groups of people to recruit. First, there are mentors for the youth. Then there are adults who help with the actual planning and leading of the confirmation class. There are teams to handle logistics, such as food, transportation, and supplies.

Finally, there are "occasional teams." These are persons with special expertise or skills whom you may use only once or twice during the time of confirmation preparation. Their schedules won't allow them to be a full-time member of the teaching team, but they will give time for special events or topics. Such persons include the music director, a resident artist, a psychologist, someone who works with service agencies in the community and can talk about mission in real terms.

When recruiting persons to work with youth, especially in confirmation, hold your standards high. These are some important qualities:

- Adults who are comfortable being adults! Youth don't need more "pals." They need someone who is willing to relate to them as an adult;
- Mentors and teachers who are able to be honest about their own faith—the deep commitments, the honest doubts, the questions;
- Adults who do not have all the answers, but are always willing to struggle with the questions. Such people are invaluable team members;
- Adults who are good listeners, but also persons who can talk honestly and openly about faith and life. They can ask questions that help others think about the meaning of their faith;
- Adults who are willing to grow in their own faith and understanding;
- Adults who have a significant faith journey of their own;
- Adults who have been a part of the church for a long enough period of time that we know something about who they are and where they stand;
- Adults who know something about the core doctrines of the church.

Everything else, you can teach adult volunteers. And that includes the skills they need for teaching/leading the class.

How do we recruit these wonderful people?

Rule No. 1: You can't start too early. Begin recruiting teachers six months before the class is scheduled to begin (July, if the class begins in January). Recruit mentors three months before the class is scheduled to begin. If someone says, "I just can't do that this year," recruit him or her on the spot for next year! And keep records, so you won't forget.

Enter the recruiting process with the stance that you are offering these people the most important thing God wants them to do in the next year. Accepting this call may be so important that you need to release them from other responsibilities in the church while they are working with confirmation.

Also operate from the stance that you expect recruits to measure up. If, in the course of conversation, you begin to get a bad feeling, check it out. Is this person not the one you want? Many churches are now adopting policies aimed at protecting children and youth, so they screen all people who work with youth.

Rule No. 2: At the beginning of the confirmation class, commission or publicly recognize teachers, mentors, support teams, and occasional teams in the Sunday morning worship service. These people are acting as representatives of the congregation in ministry; so it is appropriate both that they be recognized and that the congregation be asked to support them.

OK, we "got 'em." How do we train them?

In Chapter 4 (pages 117–121) is a model for training people as mentors. This model assumes that you, or another member of the leadership team, will lead the mentors through this training and brief them on the ways your church will support and nurture them. It's important to remember that mentors are not teachers; they are co-learners with the youth. They are "friends in faith."

Training for teachers takes a bit more time. Here's one way to do it:

Begin three to four months ahead of time. Invite teachers to an evening in your home or your study at church. Talk with them about the importance of confirmation, the theology of confirmation, and why you want them to help teach. Distribute copies of the resource you'll be using (*Claim the Name: Confirmation Teaching Plans for 6–15 Weeks* and/or *Teaching Plans for 39 Weeks*); ask the teachers to browse through it before your next meeting.

At the second meeting, begin blocking out the sessions. Make a chart, showing all the dates the class will meet. What topics will you cover in which session? When will you do retreats, field trips, and so on?

In the third meeting, begin planning specific sessions. You may want to do this in smaller teams, assigning each team a topic and asking them to work on planning how they will lead that session. Early in this meeting, do a "walk-through" of the resource, so that everyone is on the same page about how to use the resource, how to choose among options, and how to teach. Ask each team to turn in an outline of their session plan for review. (If you have only two to three persons besides yourself, you already have a small team and can get right into it.)

As part of the leadership training, study the biblical texts used in the teaching resource. Also review some of the core doctrines of the church.

You don't have to have every session planned and prepared before the confirmation class begins; but it would be helpful if the planning were done for at least the first month, and you can continue to plan about a month ahead. Working in advance allows you to give plenty of notice to support teams and occasional team members about their involvement in the class.

As part of the leadership training, study the biblical texts used in the teaching resource. Review some of the core doctrines of the church. Give the leaders a list of youth who will be in confirmation and ask them to pray for those youth by name.

Support teams probably need only an orientation session about what will be expected of them. These are the people who handle logistics and supplies. Help them get organized about who will take what responsibility. Designate one person to be the liaison with the teaching team, and to communicate specific needs to others on the support team. (One person on the teaching team might also be designated as liaison with the support team and occasional team.)

Occasional team members don't need a training session as such, but they do need to know several weeks in advance when you need their help with the class. They also need to know the purpose of the session, what else will be happening, how much time they have, and how their contribution will help make the session a success.

OK, we got 'em, and we got 'em trained. Now what?

Nurture of volunteers is critical. Show lots of appreciation. Check with them on a regular basis, to see if the process is working. Ask what help they need to do a better job. You will be meeting regularly with teachers for planning and evaluation. In those meetings, emphasize what is going well. Work on improving what could be better. Deal with questions about content and process.

> **Nurture of volunteers is critical. Show lots of appreciation. Check with them on a regular basis.**

Meet with mentors, or have another person on the leadership team meet with mentors, every month or six weeks, just to check signals.

You may choose to make name badges for each volunteer. The badge should be durable, with a solid way of attaching it to clothing. It should include the person's name, the words *Claim the Name: Confirmation*, and how he or she is a part of the confirmation program (teaching team, mentor, support team, occasional team). Invite the volunteers to wear the badges whenever they are in the church.

Ask an adult Sunday school class, the United Methodist Women, United Methodist Men, or the education work area to host a dinner or a party to honor all the volunteers in your confirmation program. On confirmation Sunday, after you list the names of all the youth being confirmed, list the names of all the people on your teams who worked with them. Ask the congregation to thank each of them personally for their work. Include them in the receiving line after the service.

Big Decisions

No, these are not *the big decisions* about lifetime commitment. These are the decisions that you have to make as you plan for confirmation in your congregation. You have already made some of them. You've set goals for confirmation, you know what you want to do, you've identified the teaching styles that are most comfortable for you, developed a teaching team, and so on. These decisions are the "practical," logistical ones you need to make to be sure everything runs smoothly.

Who Is Responsible for Confirmation?

If confirmation is a repeatable rite, and if confirmation training needs to take place on a regular basis, who is responsible for making it all happen?

The answer? *Good question.*

Churches need to wrestle with the issue and come to some understanding of who is responsible. Is the pastor to be "in charge"? Is the pastor to be a member of a team? Is the pastor to take some responsibility with certain age levels while other people take the lead in others? And what if the pastor is not as skilled an educator as other members of the congregation? These questions beg for serious attention. Conversations among the education work area, the pastor, other staff members (if any), and the staff-parish committee could address these critical questions and work out the answers in an atmosphere of collegiality.

In many United Methodist churches, the pastor may be the only staff person. In these churches, a team of laypersons could be put together to work with the pastor in leading confirmation.

A reminder: *The Book of Discipline, 1996,* clearly states that the *church* is responsible for providing children with the training necessary for them to grow into a "personal commitment to Jesus Christ as Lord and Savior." However, the pastor is responsible for *organizing* the confirmation program (Paragraph 227.4). Although the pastor does not have to lead it all (which is why I would put together a team), the pastor *is* still responsible.

What Is the Right Age?

In the past, we tended to answer this question in terms of cognitive development: Youth needed to be old enough to handle abstract thinking. This was the correct answer when we were operating out of an information model, giving youth "what they need to know," or "what they haven't learned up to now." So the answer we gave was seventh or eighth grade. Roman Catholic leaders in confirmation are pushing for "later and longer" again because they feel that it is important for youth to be able to handle abstract ideas. Some Lutherans are also moving confirmation to later in adolescence.

However, we know that discipleship does not depend on intellectual attainment. Youth are affirming the faith into which they were baptized and making a commitment to live that faith in new ways.

> **We know that discipleship does not depend on intellectual attainment.**

On the other hand, some United Methodists, particularly in the South, are pushing for confirmation as young as fourth grade, primarily in response to Southern Baptists who receive youth into membership as young as third and fourth grade. Theologically, we recognize that United Methodists become members of the church in baptism; so confirmation is dealing with an issue other than membership.

So what is the right age?

First, a practical theological note. If one becomes a member of the church in baptism (Baptismal Covenants I and II), then we are free to look at confirmation as a time for affirming faith and growing in discipleship.

Second, we saw in the section on the youth we teach (pages 70–73) a review of Westerhoff's understanding of "faith styles." The practical implications for confirmation are these:

1. The affiliative faith style reminds us that issues of belonging are so critical for youth. Early adolescence is a key time for building faith commitments based on the need of youth to belong. So we need to do confirmation in early adolescence, with a focus on discipleship and the implications of belonging to a church family. What does it mean to be a United Methodist Christian?

   Teach the skills necessary to be part of a church family: the importance of worship, the sacraments, learning, stewardship, mission, and ministry.

   Help youth understand that they are professing the faith of the church and becoming part of a faith community that goes back two thousand years. This is a level of belonging that we don't often tap.

2. A second, and different, confirmation process should be made available when youth in high school are caught up in a searching, or questioning, faith style. This time the emphasis is on doctrine. This is more than just a time to "catch" all those youth who were not confirmed in early adolescence. It is a

time to help youth rethink their faith and their commitment to that faith. This is the time to get cognitive and deal with the tricky questions in depth. What does the faith mean for youth as they get ready to graduate and go out on their own? A reaffirmation of faith would be an appropriate rite of passage/commitment as youth prepare to leave high school.

So what is the right age for confirmation? That depends, in large part, on what you decide you want to do in confirmation. But as Joshua said, "as for me and my house. . . ." I would do a multi-tier confirmation model. I would focus on belonging in early adolescence, and I would emphasize doctrine and faith exploration in later adolescence/young adulthood.

How Could I Get My Congregation to Accept a Multilevel Plan?

Many churches may feel that getting the youth involved in confirmation for just a few weeks in the sixth or seventh grade is quite an acccomplishment.

Moving beyond the minimum time period will take some creative education of the congregation, the youth, and their parents. What we're proposing is a whole new way of looking at confirmation in The United Methodist Church. It will take time and effort to "sell" it to the congregation. But you also have some important assets to help you in your selling:

● You are enthusiastic about the new model and want to make it work;
● The United Methodist Church is rethinking the meaning of confirmation; so there are lots of resources, publicity, and other tools to help you get the idea across;
● Adults, especially parents, want the best for the youth of your church. It's just that often they have not been offered a vision of what the best could be, so they're willing to settle for less;
● Youth are asking questions about the faith and what it means for their lives.

I never cease to be amazed at both the variety and the depth of questions youth raise. At a recent denominational youth gathering, I was leading a workshop on United Methodist doctrine. Youth were asking all kinds of deep questions *and* taking notes on our conversation. One young lady said in her evaluation, "This proves that youth want to deal with faith at a deep level." Challenging youth to that kind of depth can be one of your greatest assets. It is also a compelling reason for having a multi-tier confirmation program.

How do you sell the idea of a multi-tier confirmation, even with these assets? Begin by meeting with youth heading for confirmation, along with their parents. Tell them what your dream is, and why you dream it. Stress the importance of tailoring confirmation to the faith styles of youth. Point out the benefits for youth as they grow in their faith. Then you can point out the cost in time and effort, and challenge people to make that kind of commitment.

Most parents, given enough information, will rise to the challenge. Talk with the key decision-makers in the congregation to win their support. With parents and key decision-makers on your side, you have it made. You're ready to move on to the next question.

How Long Should Confirmation Last?

United Methodists are all over the map in their response to this question. In states such as Wisconsin and Minnesota, where there is a strong Lutheran culture, confirmation lasts at least a year, and sometimes two or three years. Many churches across the United States are moving to a 39-week, school-year-long confirmation program, usually at either sixth-or seventh-grade Sunday school. Other pastors and congregations want to do confirmation in four to six weeks.

What's the right answer? Again, it all depends on what you said you want to do in confirmation. How long will it take to reach the goals you have set?

What's the right answer? Again, it all depends on what you said you want to do in confirmation. How long will it take to reach the goals you have set? Can you do all you want in four weeks? Then go for it! Do you need longer than four weeks to do what you really want? Then plan for more time. No "right" answer fits every situation. You have to determine what you want to do in confirmation, and then decide how much time you need to do it.

It is fair to say, however, that building community is difficult to do in a short period of time, no matter how well you may do with content.

How Will I Ever Find the Time to Do All That?

Put it this way: If you had the opportunity to meet on a weekly basis with six to sixty adults, all of whom were eager to learn about the faith and what it means to be a United Methodist and how they could make a deeper commitment to Christ and the church, would you find the time? If you had the opportunity to meet on a weekly basis with fifteen to thirty adult members of your congregation who asked you to help them think deeply about theological questions, would you find the time?

If we can make the time for adults, we can make time for youth. These are people who are hungry for the faith and eager to make commitments.

So where *do* you find the time? You take another look at your priorities and make adjustments. If you are a pastor or staff person, get the agreement and support of the staff-parish committee to miss some other meetings and not make as many pastoral calls so you can free up the time to lead youth in faith discovery. You also take the time to recruit and train other adults to help, so that not all the responsibility, and not all the time, is on your shoulders.

What Should We Require for Confirmation?

First, you should expect that confirmation is not an "extra" in the life of youth, or that of the congregation. It is a core process for everyone involved.

Usually the question about requirements centers on attendance and/or "homework." Should we require youth to attend every session? Should we require them to attend Sunday school and worship during confirmation? (Which assumes that they wouldn't attend otherwise, but that is another problem.) Should we expect youth to read or work on assignments between sessions of the confirmation class?

The answer to the attendance question depends, in part, on when your class meets. If you meet every Sunday for a year during the Sunday school hour, perfect attendance is probably an unrealistic expectation. If you meet in retreat settings, and have only five meetings, then attendance becomes more of an issue. I used the retreat model in two different congregations, and insisted that the youth be present for every session. I would allow them to come a half hour late, or leave a half hour early, if there were conflicts. Beyond those exceptions, if they missed, they were expected to participate in a separate make-up session. This was not a punishment, but a way of keeping them involved. Any requirements need to be clearly communicated to parents in the beginning so that church and family can work together.

So there are questions you need to answer before you decide what you will or will not require: When do you meet? How many sessions of the class will you have? How important is attendance to you?

What about homework? In an ideal world, you could make assignments for outside reading and projects. In some ways, assigning homework for confirmation is like teaching a pig to sing. It irritates the pig and frustrates you!

For younger adolescents, I would limit "homework" to things they do with their parents and mentors, such as the conversations in the *Claim the Name: TalkPoints* books. Or as another example, have the teens' parents tell them the story of their baptism (or explain why they were not baptized as infants). Or have mentors and youth work together on a service project.

With older adolescents, you may find that they will self-assign more reading, or interviews with adults, or other "homework" activities. If this happens, rejoice; but don't feel like a failure if it doesn't happen.

Should We Say Confirmation "Class," or "Program"?

On the one hand, the language of "class" has roots in our denominational culture. (John Wesley had class meetings as a basic method in Methodism.) The downside of the "class" language, however, is that it implies the informational model, where it's important to assimilate a certain amount of data. Some pastors carry this model to the extreme of having an "oral exam" in the worship service to show the congregation how much the confirmands have learned. Usually, the youth are terrified; and the experience deters younger observers from ever wanting to be involved in confirmation. In addition, one can "graduate" from a class, which is not the direction we want to go. The upside is that "class" also implies structure, accountability, and expectations.

The "program" language implies more of an ongoing process, where you offer a variety of experiences and use a variety of learning styles. A program feels more open-ended than a class. However, the choice is yours.

Checklist

for Pastors and Other Leaders of Confirmation

Here's a checklist to help you deal with the "Have I thought of everything?" panic attack. This checklist assumes that you've thought through your goals for confirmation and answered the "big questions."

___ Are all the confirmation-related dates established and placed on the church calendar? (This includes the date for the service of confirmation. Parents need this on their calendars early.)
___ Are the letters of invitation mailed?
___ Are all the resources ordered?
___ Are the mentors recruited?
___ Are support teams in place?
___ Are the mentors trained (or is the date set for their training)?
___ Are articles written for the church newsletter?
___ Are your teaching plans outlined?
___ Is your teaching team (if you use one) in place and working?
___ Is the training for the teaching team complete?
___ Are parents invited to the orientation meeting? (You will have to remind them later, but it's important to get the date on their calendars.)
___ Have you planned a follow-up program for older youth who have been confirmed?
___ Are the arrangements made for your retreat(s)?
    ___ housing
    ___ transportation
    ___ permission slips
    ___ insurance
    ___ counselors (if you don't have a teaching team. Even if you do have a team, you may want additional counselors to handle cabin time, so that teachers can focus on their own tasks.)

There! Now, you don't have to worry. It's all down on paper.

What About Leadership?

Some pastors (or other leaders) prefer to do all the planning and leading of the confirmation program themselves. This simplifies planning, but it raises some other issues. For risk management, it's best to always have two adults present in any session in which you meet with youth. In addition, having only one leader, or even two, reduces the number of faith models to whom youth can relate. A larger leadership team allows more possibilities for youth to relate to adults whose style is compatible with that particular youth. A larger leadership team also spreads the teacher/leader load, makes possible more work in small groups, and provides for more adults who can relate to a particular teaching/learning style.

The last point is significant. Recent research has indicated there are at least seven significant ways in which people learn. (See "Ways Youth Learn," page 74.) Not every adult is comfortable leading activities that relate to each of those ways of learning. A larger leadership team opens the possibility for every youth to learn something in the way he or she learns best. It also opens the possibility for leaders to shine in their specialty. For example, if your group were to do a nature walk as part of a spiritual life retreat, who better than a forester, conservation agent, or environmental activist to lead it?

Mentors are also an important part of your leadership team. They may not lead in the sessions, but their relationships with youth are crucial as they help youth grow in faith maturity. Mentors should meet with the leadership team at least occasionally. They bring insights on what's happening in the lives of youth. They can suggest ways the leaders can adapt or adjust the program to meet specific spiritual, interactive, or cognitive needs of youth.

When Should We Meet?

The schedule depends, in part, on your goals for confirmation. It also depends on who the youth in the confirmation program are and on the availability of other adults in your leadership team. Let's look at some of the variables.

How available are your youth? If all your youth attend one school, you have more options for meeting times than if they attend a number of schools. The possibility of a weekday afternoon or evening is more realistic if you have only one school schedule to work around. If your youth attend many schools, your

---

options are far more limited. In the latter situation, Sunday morning during the Sunday school hour may be the best option.

Another possibility is to meet one Saturday a month from 9 A.M. to 3 P.M. It may be possible for families to schedule around one Saturday, rather than a weekly non-Sunday-morning time. Also consider scheduling the sessions for the benefit of any blended families who might be involved, in which case meeting every other week might be more appropriate. In an extended period, you can actually have more learning time than in six one-hour sessions, because you don't have to re-start every hour. You can also tackle issues in more depth, and create time for field trips. You will need to plan more carefully for extended sessions, because you will cover more material in less time than you thought possible.

Plan with the leadership team for the best possible option for your congregation. Start your planning early, several months before the first meeting with youth. The more time you allow for planning, the fewer problems you will have in the program itself.

Building Blocks for Confirmation

In a multi-tiered approach to confirmation, you can include more content, more events and experiences, more avenues of service, and more issues than was possible when we put all our eggs in the seventh-grade confirmation basket. For example, if you follow the model presented in this book, **a key building block** will be a confirmation program for early adolescents. The emphasis will be on belonging, what it means to be a United Methodist, and the skills one needs to be a fully participating member of the church.

A second key building block will be a confirmation program for late adolescents/young adults (including all those who affirmed their faith in early adolescence) with an emphasis on theology and practice.

A third building block might be a series of retreats set up as part of the total youth ministry program. These retreats would reinforce the learning of the first confirmation process and help lay the groundwork for the second period of confirmation at the end of high school. Of course, the ingredients of each of these building blocks would be present at every level.

The Language of the Church

This is the "technical vocabulary" issue, which we looked at briefly when we considered how to help youth grow in faith maturity (pages 52–53). A key part of identity as a United Methodist is knowing the language United Methodists speak, including terms such as *prevenient grace, justification, sanctification, holiness, faith and works,* and *Christian conversation.* Reclaiming Wesleyan language is not an exercise in trying to hold on to the past; it is a contribution to the future of the church.

Every profession, every skill, every group, has an "insider" language that helps build the identity of that group. Helping youth reclaim the insider language of United Methodism strengthens their sense of identity with the church. This fact is important for those of us who believe in the importance of the continuing existence of United Methodism.

People who stand in the Wesleyan tradition have a contribution to make to the life of the ecumenical community. But we can best make that contribution if we understand our own heritage. Using the language that is particular to us facilitates that understanding.

Reclaiming Wesleyan language is also important for those of us who believe in helping youth deal with the pressures of living in the post-modern world. Surprisingly enough, identification with a denomination is one factor that helps youth avoid high-risk behavior (according to Boys Town research). Another way to say that is that denominational identification helps create life patterns and habits that are sustaining. Speaking our own language makes that creation easier.

> **The heart of the Christian faith is relationships. We are called into relationship with God in Jesus Christ. We are called to know God, as well as know about God.**

Relationships

The heart of the Christian faith is relationships. We are called into relationship with God in Jesus Christ. We are called to *know* God, as well as *know about* God. We are called into relationships with one another. These relationships begin in the family, and then grow to include the family of God.

John Wesley was insistent that "the New Testament knows no solitary religion." We are called, in our baptism, into a community of believers. Jesus said that the Great Commandment was love for God and love for neighbor. The "neighbor" is more than just the person who lives next door, or even the people we see at church on Sunday. The "neighbor" is everyone we meet, every person in need, every situation that calls for love and compassion.

Relationships suggest two important goals: wholeness and faith maturity. God calls us to be whole, healthy human beings. In theological terms, we are called to "go on to perfection," with perfection defined as wholeness, or completion.

On one plane, youth need basic life skills in order to be whole. If they cannot cope with life, they cannot grow in discipleship. For example, Search Institute has identified forty assets that are important in order for children and youth to grow into healthy human beings. Youth also need spiritual skills—the support of the community of faith, a vital spiritual discipline, knowledge of the content of the faith—to become whole.

Closely related to wholeness is faith maturity. (See pages 47–53.) Faith maturity is built on relationships, grows out of relationships, and leads to deeper relationships with God and the people of God.

A key to confirmation, then, is the relationships we nurture among youth. We help youth grow in relationship with God and with one another. We help teach skills for relationships, and try to facilitate the vertical relationship as much as possible. As leaders develop relationships with youth—built on mutual trust and caring—we model Christian discipleship and open the doors for deeper relationships with God.

Sessions

Once you have decided how many sessions your confirmation program will include and when and where the sessions will be held, you begin to look at how each session is structured.

Many of us, who are content-oriented and feeling pressed for time (actually, that may be most of us), want to jump right in. "OK, it's time to quiet down and get started," is the traditional model for many sessions. We also close with "I guess that's it for today. See you next week," or "Well, your parents are starting to arrive, so we'll stop." It is important, however, to take time for relationship-building. If we begin each session with a time of community-gathering and end with prayer or a benediction, we provide a structure for the session that offers comfort to youth who may be uneasy about all the new "stuff" that's coming at them. These "bookends" for the session also help set the confirmation process in a context of spiritual discipline. As a fringe benefit, an opening time for community often helps "settle kids down," and we can actually move into content quicker and easier.

The *Claim the Name* resources for younger adolescents (both the 6–15-week model and the 39-week model) include both community-gathering and closing worship or benediction elements for each confirmation session. One resource uses basically the same pattern every week. The other uses a different pattern and different activities almost every week, but the basic community time is in the session plan. You can adapt either or both to fit your situation.

Content

While relationship is at the heart of the faith, content is also important. What we teach does make a difference. We have said, in the multi-tier approach to confirmation, that the faith affirmed in confirmation is the faith of the church, symbolized by the Apostles' Creed. In many ways, the words of that creed (and of the Nicene Creed, the other historic creed printed in *The United Methodist Hymnal*) provide a framework for the content we teach. They include the mighty acts of God in history, the life and work of Jesus the Christ, the relationships among the Trinity, the church, baptism, forgiveness of sins, resurrection of the body, and life eternal.

What we teach does make a difference. The words of the creeds provide a framework for our content.

As United Methodists we also want to include our history; the history of the church at large; and our unique contributions to theology, music, and mission in the church. A wide variety of learning activities and experiences will help youth gain access to the content and incorporate it into their lives.

Content is important. The *Book of Discipline* recognizes this reality when it says that only United Methodist resources should be used for confirmation. Our history shapes our practice, our practice shapes our formation, our formation affects our relationship with Jesus Christ and what we understand about ourselves. So yes, content matters.

Retreats

----------------------->

Do we include retreats as a part of our confirmation program? Fifty-one percent of United Methodist churches do, according to research conducted by The United Methodist Publishing House.

● Retreats model Jesus' practice of setting time apart for spiritual renewal.
● Retreats allow youth to escape the pressures of their daily "grind" and have time to relax. Retreats are settings in which the work of building a community of youth with youth, youth with adults, and all participants with Jesus Christ can go on in some depth.
● Retreats provide extended periods to practice spiritual disciplines. Moving outside the pattern of daily living to a new setting can help each of us open up to learning more deeply.
● Retreats also allow for both experience and reflection, two learning models that are crucial for the millennial generation, according to studies done by the General Board of Discipleship.

Retreats do require extra work in planning, preparation, and logistics, including cost. You will need to budget for retreats, as a part of your planning. Adults, mentors, and team leaders may be needed for planning, teaching, food preparation, cleanup, and more. If you have twenty or fewer youth, meal preparation and cleanup—working side by side with adults—can be additional time for community-building. This becomes more difficult in a large group, because there are not enough opportunities for every youth to participate.

Many confirmation experiences include two retreats: one at the beginning of the process to build community and begin the practice of spiritual disciplines, and the other at the end of the confirmation process, to reflect on the meaning of the shared experience and to make commitments for the future.

Some churches use the retreat model as a key ingredient of their confirmation program. *Claim the Name: Retreats for Continuing the Journey* provides four retreat opportunities in each of the age levels of grades 6–8, grades 9–10, and grades 11–12. The four retreats' themes are consistent across the age levels and consistent with key elements of confirmation: Being God's People, Following Jesus, Living as United Methodists, and Walking the Talk.

Field Trips

Field trips allow youth to actually participate in worship and/or conversation with people of other denominations or other faith traditions. Trips to a synagogue, a Roman Catholic or Eastern Orthodox worship service, followed by a time of conversation with the rabbi or priest, can open the eyes of youth to other worship traditions, other ways of expressing one's faith, and to the importance of being open to those who believe and worship differently.

Visits to other United Methodist churches may introduce youth to the variety of worship styles that are a part of our own tradition. They also help youth experience being a part of the larger connection.

Field trips to United Methodist agencies/ministries let youth see firsthand some ways United Methodists work together for mercy and justice in the world. These trips also help youth experience the power of the "connection" in United Methodism. Trips to United Methodist historic sites, where this is possible, give youth a sense of their roots.

All trips need to be planned carefully, in consultation with the host for the experience, so that both your leaders and your hosts are clear about the purpose of the event. Spiritual leaders in other faith communities want to be assured that you are not visiting as tourists, but as pilgrims seeking to grow in faith. They will be more open to talking about their traditions if they are a part of the teaching/learning process, rather than tour guides.

Staff at United Methodist agencies can be more helpful to your group if they know exactly why you are visiting and what you hope your youth will learn. Community-serving agencies could help you develop a project where your youth actually work for the agency. Then they can talk with the agency staff about their experience, learning how the agency serves the community.

Mission/Service Projects

Consider these points as you think about service projects:

First, all service needs to be meaningful, introducing youth to human need and showing them that they can make a difference. Three hours in a food bank or homeless shelter would be far more significant than a day spent cleaning the church.

Second, all service is in a context. Prepare the youth for what they will be doing, and why it is important. Youth who have led relatively sheltered, comfortable lives may be uncomfortable or uneasy when interacting with persons who are homeless or ill. Be very clear with the youth about what they can expect (without frightening them). Help them deal with their feelings.

Third, make careful preparations. Be sure the people in charge understand the nature of your group and how they can assist in making the service meaningful.

Fourth, all service needs to conclude with time for reflection. What happened? What did it mean to the youth? What did it mean to people who were helped by the project? What does all of that have to do with God?

Spiritual Disciplines

Why should we even talk about "spiritual disciplines" or "practicing the faith"? Isn't it enough just to believe?

Well, let's think for a minute about how we become good at anything. How does one become a starter on the basketball team? By practicing. Taking shots, over and over. Running, lifting weights, playing the game. Watching for mistakes and correcting them, until every play is executed, almost automatically, the right way. How does one make first chair in the band, or become an accomplished pianist? By practicing. Playing scales over and over, doing simple exercises, then harder ones, then tackling the music. Doing it over and over, until the music isn't even necessary anymore.

You get the point. How does one become a Christian? How does one mature in faith? How does one "go on to perfection"? By practicing how to be a Christian. That's what the spiritual disciplines are all about. They are ways we practice the faith until it becomes a part of us. We develop life habits that help us make choices, creating patterns that reflect our growing relationship with Christ.

What are spiritual disciplines? Maybe the best place to begin is with John Wesley and what he called "works of piety" and "works of mercy." These aren't the only spiritual disciplines, but they are a good beginning point for United Methodists. Mr. Wesley wrote a little guide for Christian living that he called "The Nature, Design, and General Rules, of the United Societies." Today these are found in "The General Rules of The Methodist Church" (pages 69–72 of *The Book of Discipline, 1996*).

Works of Piety

In the General Rules that Wesley laid out for the United Societies, he said that we are to "[attend] upon all the ordinances of God." In other places, he said that we should use all the "means of grace." Wesley said that means of grace are "outward signs, words, or actions, ordained of God" to be the "ordinary channels" through which grace is conveyed to us (Sermon #16, "The Means of Grace"). God works in other ways as well, but these are the "ordinary ways" in which God works. Dwight Vogel describes the means of grace as those places where God meets us "by previous appointment" (*By Water and the Spirit: A Study of Baptism for United Methodists*; Cokesbury, 1993; page 9).

These means of grace include

● **The public worship of God.** Every Sunday morning we have a "previous appointment" with God. Even when the sermon is dull, the music is out-of-date, and the pews are too hard, God is present. Regular worship is a part of the "practice field" of the faith. We may not always be inspired, but we are always in the presence of God and we learn how to recognize God's presence.

Does that mean we should require youth in the confirmation class to attend worship every Sunday? Not necessarily, but I have to admit I can't understand why anyone would want to become part of an organization whose meetings they never attend. If we want to grow in our relationship to God, we need to be present to Christ; and the practice of worship is a key way to do that.

● **The ministry of the Word,** either read or expounded. This means listening to the preaching or teaching of the Bible. Part of that happens in worship, part in Sunday school, part in special classes, such as Youth DISCIPLE or the Wednesday night Bible study. Great changes have happened in individual lives and in the life of the church because of the Bible, but people had to be reading the Bible first.

Do we need to have in-depth Bible study in confirmation? Not necessarily, though we would hope that the confirmation process is firmly grounded in Scripture. The Sunday school is the primary setting where children and youth are learning the stories of the Bible and how to use such tools for Bible study as a concordance, an atlas, Bible dictionaries, and commentaries. In confirmation education, we build on work already done, and use the Bible to lead us to a deeper knowledge of the faith.

- **The Supper of the Lord.** This is part of Sunday worship, but deserves special attention. Wesley said that the sacrament is a means by which God gives us either prevenient, justifying, or sanctifying grace, depending on our need at the moment. It is a time of special awareness of God.

One question youth often raise is, "But I didn't feel anything different. Did I do something wrong? Was God not there?" Remind them that God is always present. Encourage them to practice listening for Christ in the sacrament. Rehearsing the work of Christ with people through the ages and now extended to us shapes us as a part of Christ's people.

- **Family and private prayer.** Part of faith maturity is the vertical relationship with God. Keeping any relationship alive and growing takes time and effort. My wife and I have many friends all over the country, many of whom we don't see for years at a time. We keep the relationships open and growing through letters, phone calls, and e-mail. We also have to work at keeping the relationship with God open and growing. In this relationship, prayer takes the place of letters and phone calls.

Prayer definitely should be a part of the confirmation process. Adults (leaders, pastors, mentors, parents) should model the practice of prayer, but not do all the praying. Build in times for youth to pray—silently and also aloud, during worship.

- **Searching the Scriptures.** This is different from listening to sermons or doing Bible study. This is what happens when we sit down and read the Bible, seeking to grow in faith, to hear a personal word from God. An important part of confirmation education should be helping youth develop skills in Bible reading and learn how to listen for God as they read.

- **Fasting or abstinence.** Wesley was sure that fasting was an important spiritual discipline, but only when one fasted for the sake of God. He did not believe in fasting as a weight-loss program or as "giving up something for Lent" (and then binging come Easter). He thought fasting was a way to focus the body and the mind on God and should be used only as one part of a turning to God. He definitely believed in abstinence (from alcohol and tobacco, for example) as a spiritual discipline that helps us keep our focus on God and not on our cravings or addictions.

Because of the emphasis on thinness in our society, the obsession with diets, and the dangers of anorexia or bulimia, I only rarely recommend fasting. Those instances would be as part of a spiritual-life retreat in which the group agreed to fast for a limited time, with a definite purpose in mind. Abstinence, however—

from anything that is a habit and can get in the way of good physical or spiritual health—is always appropriate. Even more appropriate is to consider the way we commit the abstinence to God, as a spiritual discipline, or means of grace.

● **Christian conversation.** John Wesley thought this was so important that he organized class meetings to provide a vehicle for it to happen. Meeting with other Christians in a small group does at least three things for each person in the group. First, we discover that we are not alone in the life of faith. Second, we find encouragement and support for our faith journey. Third, and perhaps the most important, we become accountable to others for our Christian journey.

Accountability is not an easy concept in a culture that revels in individualism, freedom, and "I can do whatever I want." But accountability is an important way for us to grow in our faith and in our relationships with others. Providing youth with friends in faith, whether they be mentors or peers, is also a way to encourage Christian conversation.

More Works of Piety

This, then, was the Wesleyan model. Other disciplines can also be means of grace for us. They include, but are not limited to

● stewardship
● writing in journals (Wesley did this all through his life.)
● confirmation itself

Let's look at each of these:

● **Stewardship** is both a discipline and a way of life. The membership vows of The United Methodist Church say we will uphold our church by our prayers, our presence, our gifts, and our service. These vows include the stewardship of our money, our talents, and our sweat equity, as well as our attendance and our prayers. All are important, and we need to promote them to youth in the confirmation process as part of the disciplines by which we grow in faith.

● **Writing in journals** is an important tool for both growing in faith and checking on our growth. When we keep a written record of our faith journey, we grow in the process of writing. We can also look back across time, see where we've been, and discover how we've grown. The personal nature of this discipline makes it easy for us to express concerns, doubts, questions, even confessions, that we might not raise in a group. Writing and rereading what we've written becomes an aid to reflection on our life with God and with others.

● **Confirmation (as process and ritual)** is a spiritual discipline and a means of grace. The multi-tiered confirmation approach that we suggest is a way to make the discipline of growing in faith a conscious part of the adolescent and young adult years. Confirmation then becomes not some class we have to endure so we can "graduate," but a journey in faith with friends and with God.

Works of Mercy

In the General Rules, Wesley described works of mercy as "doing good." We normally refer to these as good works. Wesley said that we should do good to all persons:

● First, to their bodies. This includes such things as providing food for the hungry, clothes for the naked, and shelter for the homeless. Wesley spent his life doing these things. He also provided schools for the children of the poor, opened medical clinics for those who could not afford a doctor, and so on.

Service should be an integral part of confirmation. Youth grow in faith as they work with a food bank, Room in the Inn, Habitat for Humanity, the soup kitchen at the mission, or wherever there is human need. As we prepare to serve others, we remind one another that we meet Christ in persons in need.

**Remember:
Plan time to reflect
on the experience.
What happened?
What did we
discover about God?
about faith?**

Help youth find ways to look for Christ in the faces of the hungry, the homeless, the sick. Encourage them to be as Christ for these persons. "What would Jesus do?" becomes an important question in these settings. How would Jesus deal with a hungry, homeless person who comes to a soup kitchen for one good meal a day?

Remember: Plan time to reflect on the experience. What happened? What did we discover about God? about faith?

● Second, Wesley said, we need to care for the souls of others. This includes telling stories of the faith, calling others to account when they mess up, and encouraging them to be faithful in their Christian journey. Do it all in a spirit of love. I'll never forget a twelfth-grade girl saying to a younger boy in our youth group, "What you did was totally stupid and wrong, but I love you and will stand with you while you take the consequences." That's caring for the souls of others!

Then, Wesley said, don't give in to the nonsense that "we are not to do good unless *our heart be free to it.*" That is the notion that we shouldn't do good works unless we feel good about it. How many times have we dragged ourselves to the shelter or somewhere else just because we "had to," and came home with a blessing? We can, in fact, act our way to feeling different.

Jesus reminded us of the importance of practicing our faith. Read the series of sayings about practicing piety in Matthew 6:1-6, 16-18. As you read, imagine a strange little character parading through town with his own private brass band. They see a beggar, and the little character stops to drop a coin into the beggar's cup. He reaches into his pocket. The brass band sounds off. Everyone on the street stops to look. Can't you just see it?

But that's nothing. Wait until he gets to church! When the offering plate comes around, the little character reaches for his envelope. He poises his envelope over the plate, and the whole band breaks out into a rousing "Hallelujah" chorus, with a counterpoint of "Hail, the Conquering Hero Comes."

Or prayers. Imagine this little character standing on the busiest corner of your town, just at noon when all the people from all the offices hit the street for lunch, or shopping, or errands. Here's this little guy, standing there, praying away at the top of his voice.

Jesus had some harsh things to say about people like that. But he never said they shouldn't give money, or pray, or engage in anything else that was an act of piety. He never said, Don't practice your piety. He only said, Don't practice it out in public, where everyone can see you and praise you for it. If you do, the publicity is all the good it will do you. Rather, do it "in secret."

What?

Chapter
4

What else do we do to ensure success? What are our resources?

To start with, you have wonderful people resources as well as excellent published resources. Also, here are some of the most frequently asked questions about confirmation. (What? Oh yes. There are also some answers.)

The big question, of course, is how to help youth claim the name Christian for themselves. And what if they say no? We'll address that also. Finally, we've collected some great ideas for celebrating the special day.

Get the Most From Your People Resources

Helping the Congregation Claim Confirmation

"I'd like to do more with confirmation, but I don't have the support from the congregation that I need." "Confirmation doesn't mean much to our congregation; they want to know if youth are being saved." "Last Sunday was confirmation; it didn't seem special to me. I thought the youth being confirmed were slighted by the way the service was conducted and the way the congregation responded."

Sound familiar? I get so excited about confirmation, I sometimes forget that the congregation doesn't know as much about what's going on as I do. Here are some ways you can communicate to the congregation and help them develop ownership for the confirmation program:

1. Encourage mentors to talk with other adults about what's happening in confirmation. They should not betray any confidences; but they can talk about class sessions, what they've learned, and the excitement and joy of working with youth.

2. Encourage parents to spread the word too. In one church I served, we referred to this as "gossiping the gospel." People talked about what was happening in church when they met one another in the grocery store, at work, over coffee in fellowship hall, and on the golf course.

3. Invite the congregation to participate in a special study on confirmation in your church. This study could include

● the meaning of baptism (possible resource: the study guide *By Water and the Spirit;* Cokesbury, 1993);
● the relationship of baptism and confirmation; confirmation as a repeatable rite;
● why confirmation is important for youth (see "Goals for Confirmation," pages 38–46);
● what topics you're covering in confirmation with younger adolescents;
● why it's important to have a second confirmation experience for older adolescents (see pages 72–73) and topics you cover in that experience;
● opportunity for questions and comments;
● a list of ways members of the congregation can support the confirmation program.

4. Keep the congregation informed about what's happening. You don't need to report on every session; but you can keep the confirmation process, along with the youth, in front of the congregation on a regular basis:

● Include youth in the confirmation class (and their mentors) in the pastoral prayer on a regular basis.
● Invite the congregation to pray for the youth by name.
● Print a list of youth in the confirmation class, and a list of mentors, in the church's prayer calendar.
● Preach on vocation and discipleship, using *By Water and the Spirit* and "Where We Are Today—A Theology of Baptism" (pages 26–37) as resources.

- Use illustrations from the confirmation materials to enrich the sermon(s).
- Preach on the basics of the faith, using the Apostles' Creed as an outline for the series. Illustrate the sermons with stories from the confirmation materials.
- Invite the confirmation class to make and display posters or banners about what they are doing in the class.
- Have a brief notice in the church newsletter either before or after each session of the class, noting the topics covered by that session.

5. Involve the worship work area in making banners for confirmation. One congregation began making banners for each confirmation class. The youth determined the theme of the banner. The banner, which included the full name of each member of the class, was carried in the processional on confirmation Sunday. For six weeks after that, it hung in the sanctuary as a reminder of the class, and of the congregation's commitment to the continued spiritual nurture of that class. Banners from previous classes also hung in the sanctuary for those Sundays. The last time I was in that church, there were too many banners to hang in the sanctuary; and most of them were permanently displayed on the halls of the education wing. Every person who went to a Sunday school class was reminded every Sunday of the importance of confirmation in that congregation.

6. Make confirmation Sunday a high point of worship, celebration, and commitment. There are several simple ways to do this:

- Keep the focus on the youth and their affirmation of faith/commitment. Don't add other "special" elements to that particular service.
- Find ways, such as giving gifts to each confirmand, to make this a special service. We used to call youth to the altar, one at a time, to be confirmed. The pastors, lay leader, and lay liturgist participated in the laying on of hands. The parents of that particular young person were also at the altar to present him or her with a gift (purchased by the parents, but selected by the church). Yes, we did that with forty-seven youth in the principal worship service. Sometimes we eliminated other elements in the service; but I also told the congregation for weeks ahead that this service would run long, and that they would love it.
- Have a group in the congregation (evangelism, membership care, United Methodist Women, United Methodist Men, United Methodist Youth) sponsor a reception for the confirmation class, their parents, and their mentors, immediately following the service. Place the receiving line between the exit from the sanctuary and the refreshments.

- Take lots of pictures, both of the group and of individuals, and display them prominently.
- Hold a special training session for the administrative council on ways to include youth who have finished confirmation as adult participants in the life of the church.

Meeting With Parents

The surest way to gain support for the confirmation program is to involve parents in it. If your youth was confirmed last year, and you were happy about the experience, you will be an enthusiastic "salesperson" for the confirmation program. If your youth will be confirmed next year, you will want to be sure that the confirmation program is the very best possible program. So involve the parents.

Some congregations involve parents as teachers or mentors; but in this section, we're going to assume that parents don't have that kind of "hands-on" relationship with the program. You still will find that regular meetings with parents will pay huge dividends. Hold a meeting with parents prior to the start of the confirmation class or program. This meeting should include all the information parents will need about meeting times and places, the date of the confirmation service, what topics will be covered, and any other specific information related to your program.

One year, I had two youth tell me they couldn't be at the confirmation service, because that was Memorial Day and their family always went to the lake on that weekend. Later that day, when I met with the parents and told them when the service would be and why it was important to have it on that Sunday (it was Pentecost), those parents were the first to say they would be there and even asked what they could do to help.

In many cases, parents have asked for a class for themselves, one that covered the same topics their youth were studying, so they could know enough to be able to carry on a conversation or answer questions. While providing this option could be a drain on any busy person's time, it is also one of the most effective ways to use that time. You build parental support for the confirmation class. You help parents talk intelligently with their youth about the faith. You teach parents, many of whom will be leaders in the congregation, more of the basics of the faith. That's a major payoff for your investment of time and energy. Think of ways you could include such a series in your church's program.

Speaking of parents wanting to talk with their youth, one part of your meeting with the parents should include introducing them to the resource *Claim the Name: TalkPoints for Parents and Youth*. In the meeting itself, have the parents experience a TalkPoint. (Pages 5–8 in this book contain material for a parent-to-parent conversation.) Once parents have done one TalkPoint, they are more confident in using the TalkPoints with their youth at home on their own.

It would be easier to simply send the book home and trust parents to follow through. But you'll have a higher percentage of use—and effectiveness—if you simply plan thirty minutes at the meeting for doing one TalkPoint right there. Another advantage of using the *TalkPoints* book in the parent meeting is that single parents can pair with other single parents for a conversation.

Include regular information sessions for parents. No matter what the schedule your class follows, plan for a parents' meeting once a month. Here is one possible agenda for that meeting:

● Open with prayer.
● Engage in community-building (even in a small-membership congregation, not all the parents may know one another).
● Ask for feedback: "What do you hear? What are your youth saying? How would you say we're doing?"
● Review what you've covered in the past month.
● Preview what you will cover in the next month.
● Discuss how to use *Claim the Name: TalkPoints for Parents and Youth* with youth.
● Invite questions and comments.
● Close with prayer.

Training Mentors

You have invested time in recruiting adults who want to be friends in faith and co-learners with the youth. The best way to honor their commitment and reap dividends on your investment is to give them the training and nurture they need to be successful.

Model for a Training Session

● Include dinner. Convince your mentors that they are involved in a critically important ministry. Provide the evening meal—and childcare—for this training session. With a little work, you can get parents to cater the dinner and older youth to provide the child care.

- Emphasize community-building.
- Discuss what confirmation is and why it is important (see "Where We Are Today—A Theology of Baptism," pages 26–37, and "Goals for Confirmation," pages 38–46).
- Provide an overview of who mentors are and what they do.
- Review the confirmation materials.
- Review resources for mentoring.
- Experience TalkPoints.
- Address risk-management issues.
- Hear questions and comments.
- Close with worship, with an emphasis on commitment.

Model for Ongoing Training and Nurture

- Opening prayer
- Community-building
- Check-up time:

  - How's it going?
  - What joys are you experiencing? What are your frustrations?
  - How can we (staff, other leadership) help you in your role as mentor?
  - What questions about faith and practice do you have?
  - What are some potential growth areas for your own faith that you've uncovered?

- Other questions and comments
- Closing prayer

A Long-Range Mentoring Program

When an infant is baptized, the parents, godparents, other family members, and the entire congregation, commit themselves to nurturing the child in faith. Build on that commitment for a long-range mentoring program. Godparents are, in a sense, mentors for life already. What we have to do is help them understand the reality of the commitment they have made and discover ways to live it out.

One implication is that godparents are members of the congregation.
If the parents want in-laws from halfway across the country to be godparents, that's fine. But here's a radical idea: Also have godparents from the congregation. That's non-negotiable. If, for some reason, the godparents leave the congregation and can no longer serve, they are replaced by others from the

congregation. If a family with baptized children moves into the congregation, they are assigned resident godparents.

"Do you know what you're saying? We'd spend all our time recruiting godparents. We don't have time to do mentors, let alone all this!"

Actually, I do realize exactly what it means. It means we take the Baptismal Covenant seriously and expect the congregation to take it seriously. It means we expect parents to take seriously what their child's baptism and church membership implies. It means we have to spend more time in recruiting and training. But it also means the congregation begins to take ownership of Christian nurture. In a few years, pastors can turn the recruiting and training over to laypersons, who are "on fire" for the idea, because they see it working. That means the congregation will carry on the idea long after the pastor has left that church. It also means you will never have to recruit mentors for confirmation—they are already in place.

Here are some steps to make this program work:

● Have a sermon on the importance of the commitment the parents and congregation make in the Baptismal Covenant.
● Point out that being intentional godparents is one expression of that commitment.
● Invite persons who are willing to be godparents to come to the altar at the close of the service. Set up personal interviews with these persons; be clear about their motivation. Train them. Assign them as godparents to babies who are baptized in your congregation.
● Have regular meetings with godparents to provide support and continuing education.
These should be held at least twice a year, for two to three hours. Learn how the relationships are working, what godparents need in the way of support, what resources would be helpful. If these godparents are taking their responsibility seriously, they are probably starving for more biblical, theological, and interpersonal skills.

> **With this extra effort, you are building an interdependent community of faith, a community of role models for youth, a core of people deeply committed to Christian education. You are building the body of Christ.**

With this extra effort, you are building an interdependent community of faith, as parents and godparents work together on the Christian nurture of youth. You are building a community of role models for youth, persons (in addition to their parents) with whom they can talk about life and faith. You are building a core of people who are deeply committed to a high-quality program of Christian education for children and youth. In fact, if they take you seriously, they will probably begin to demand more from the Christian education program and be more willing to support it. You are building the body of Christ, the household of faith.

Then, when confirmation comes, you have mentors in place who already have a relationship with the youth. Both are comfortable talking about faith. They trust one another. They are ready to move on to the next step.

Another Long-Range Mentoring Program

Mentors don't have to end that relationship on confirmation Sunday. They can continue relating to youth—though perhaps at less frequent intervals—right through college and into the beginning of adult life.

Here's a hypothetical case:

> **Mentors don't have to end that relationship on confirmation Sunday.**

Tom Rundberg is a mentor of Jermaine Lowry and Mark Fulbright. They go through confirmation together and develop a good relationship. Tom continues to meet with Jermaine and Mark through junior high and high school. He goes to ballgames and band concerts. They meet for "faith checkups" about once a month, usually at a fast-food place, so Jermaine and Mark can make their daily calorie quota. When the boys struggle with the complexities of relationships, Tom is there to listen. The three talk about the sermon last Sunday, what's happening in Sunday school and youth group, and how to live as a Christian in school. (Note that Tom is learning as much as the boys are.)

Then comes high school graduation. Jermaine goes off to the university; Mark goes to the local community college and works in his parents' store. Tom talks to Jermaine via e-mail at least once a week, and sees Mark about that often. When Jermaine is home, the three get together, sometimes for dinner at their favorite restaurant. Transitions are always tough for youth, but Tom helps them work through their new experiences—and relate those life changes to faith.

Later, Tom is there for Jermaine and Mark when they leave college and make adjustments to new jobs, sometimes new cities (e-mail is a wonderful thing!), and the complexities of being a Christian in the workplace. Tom and his wife are guests of honor at weddings, baptisms, and other special events.

An impossible dream? Well, a dream. And it won't always come true in as smooth a fashion as our hypothetical case. But whenever it comes true, to any degree, we have helped to build up the body of Christ. We have equipped the saints for the work of ministry (1 Corinthians 12:4-11; Ephesians 4:11-13).

Get Help From the Published Resources

Grade Level Choices

6th–8th	*Claim the Name: Confirmation Teaching Plans for 6–15 Weeks* *Claim the Name: Confirmation Teaching Plans for 39 Weeks* Five Keepsake Student Books
6th–8th 9th–10th 11th–12th	*Claim the Name: Retreats for Continuing the Journey* *Retreats* *Retreats*
11th–12th	*Faith Exploration for Older Youth and Young Adults*

Claim the Name: Confirmation Teaching Plans for 6–15 Weeks is the basic resource for short-term confirmation classes for grades six through eight. It contains material for fifteen sessions, but can be used in fewer. The introductory material suggests different ways to select from the material for a shorter series.

Claim the Name: Confirmation Teaching Plans for 39 Weeks is the basic resource for churches whose confirmation for grades six through eight lasts for the full school year.

Keepsake books replace traditional student books. These innovative little books reinforce experiences and learnings in the sessions. They are given to youth at various points in the program. They are another way of connecting youth with key information—information with the power to transform their lives. Here are the titles of the **keepsake books:**

● *What's in a Name?* (the church, Christianity, and confirmation)
● *About That Name* (being United Methodist)
● *The Name I Claim* (faith)
● *The Name Above All* (sin, salvation, and Jesus)
● *Proclaim the Name* (being confirmed)

The keepsake books are used with the *6–15 Weeks* and the *39 Weeks* confirmation resources, and are also recommended for use during the retreats. Instructions in the leader materials tell when to use the keepsake books.

Claim the Name: Retreats for Continuing the Journey provides help to the fifty-one percent of churches that regularly include one or more retreats as part of their confirmation program. Also, since it has four retreats each for grades six to eight, nine to ten, and eleven to twelve, it is a valuable addition to a multi-tier approach to confirmation. Dealing with themes common to the confirmation experience, *Retreats* can also be used as either the confirmation program itself or as a supplement at the older ages for groups who were confirmed earlier.

Faith Exploration is specifically for older youth and young adults. It builds on the searching-faith style and helps youth and young adults wrestle with questions about doctrine. The material is based on Wesleyan theology within the framework of United Methodist doctrinal standards. Bible study is integral. The learning style is a mix of experiential and reflective. Topics include God, Jesus, salvation, grace, the church, decision-making, and social justice. *Faith Exploration* is a leader's guide containing some reproducible pages. There is no separate student material. Leaders can choose from options that allow them to design from six to thirty-nine sessions.

A Visual Treasury of United Methodism. These seven colorful posters provide a wealth of information and inspiration. They are inviting, multifaceted tools that illustrate and trace our United Methodist heritage:

● The Beginnings of Methodism (John Wesley in England)
● Methodism in Early America (Francis Asbury and company)
● Making a Difference (the connectional church at work)
● Into All the World (the connectional church at work)
● Church History Tree
● Methodist History Tree
● Our United Methodist Beliefs (including our distinctive emphases)

Claim the Name: TalkPoints for Mentors and Youth. Mentors often wonder, How do I begin a conversation about faith? What do I say? Here is a tool for that situation. There is just enough structure to help adults feel comfortable in talking with youth—and vice versa. The resource contains duplicate pages—one for the mentor, one for the confirmand—so that the two can easily talk to each other about the faith. Now mentors can develop a conversation rather than ask one question after another, and youth can hold mentors accountable to the conversation as well. Ten TalkPoints are included in this resource.

Claim the Name: TalkPoints for Parents and Youth. A recent television commercial stressed the importance of adults talking to their teenagers. The "hook" was, if you spend time talking to your teens, they are less likely to do drugs. That's true, but parents are often totally baffled about how to talk to this adolescent stranger who has suddenly appeared at the dinner table. TalkPoints make it possible for both youth and parents (and other family members) to begin conversations about the faith. There are six TalkPoints, each with duplicate pages for parents and youth.

Confirmation Class Sessions–A Model

No matter how many sessions your confirmation class consists of, consider using this general outline for each session:

- Gathering: Ask each youth to rate the past week in one or two sentences;
- Silent reflection (with guidance for the youth—for example, thank God for one good thing that's happened this week; or tell God one thing you're unhappy about);
- Introductory activity for the session;
- Body of the session;
- Looking ahead to the next session/housekeeping items;
- Blessing and sending forth.

Depending on the size of your group, you will need to adapt some of these elements. For example, with a large class, do the gathering and silent reflection in small groups. The key to this model is that it is not resource-dependent. You can use it with any resource.

What Do We Do? FAQ's

What is the "right age" for confirmation?

Our understanding of faith development suggests that early adolescence (sixth or seventh grade) is a good time for the first stage of confirmation. Here the emphasis is on belonging, identity, and the skills necessary to be a part of the church. Later adolescence (eleventh or twelfth grade) is a good time for dealing with more abstract theological ideas as part of the searching/questioning faith style in which older youth find themselves. So what is the right time for confirmation? Both early and late adolescence, with an emphasis on the word *both*.

How do we get older youth to "do confirmation again"?

One youth worker told me about introducing this concept to her twelfth graders. She said, "It's going to be confirmation for older youth." They said, "We've already done confirmation. That's for little kids; we don't want to do it again." So she said, "OK, it's not confirmation. We're going to dig into what we believe." They said, 'OK, that's cool." On the other hand, my senior highs said recently, "We need to do confirmation again, so we can ask the right questions."

How do you get older youth involved?

- Talk to them, either individually or in a group. Lay out what you'd like to do: help them think about their faith in more adult ways before they graduate;
- Get past the "confirmation is for little kids" barrier. Tell them confirmation is a time of preparation for professing our faith, no matter what our age;
- Make a covenant to explore what the faith means in adult terms. *Faith Exploration* is designed to do this with older youth. The content is on an adult level, but the process is interactive;
- Put major effort into the confirmation class for older youth. This could be the foundation for reaching unchurched youth for years to come and a "refresh-and-go-deeper" for youth who were confirmed at a younger age.
- Make the service of confirmation and/or reaffirmation of baptism for these youth a "big deal." They deserve being able to profess their faith with as much ritual and excitement as do younger youth.

We have trouble getting kids to confirmation regularly. Family schedules, and especially two households, make regular attendance difficult. Any ideas?

Here's where the parent meeting is so important. Invite *all* parents to that meeting, not just the one who is the primary caregiver. Present the importance of the confirmation process, of regular attendance, and of commitment to the process. Ask for the parents' help. Even ex-spouses who are still angry with each other will often make an effort to cooperate for the sake of their children. Also, giving busy families a schedule well in advance is helpful, as is keeping up your communication to parents about what's happening. The families then have the information—and the encouragement—to make confirmation a priority.

We don't have enough youth. What do we do?

Try having confirmation every other year, or every third year. Think long-term. Are there a lot of fourth graders and only one fifth grader? Know that, a year from now, you will need to talk to your fifth grader and her family and encourage them to wait a year, so she and the six youth a year behind her can form a large enough group to make a variety of activities possible. Consider also joining with another nearby church for shared classes and leadership. Or go ahead with a small number at your church, but also take advantage of district or conference confirmation events; or invite one or two older youth who have been confirmed to participate again as a part of their ministry to the younger youth.

How do we help youth take the confirmation process seriously without having to exclude one or two troublemakers?

Here's where having a team helps. With a leadership team, one adult can work directly with the "troublemakers" and help them grow in their sense of belonging and responsibility to the group. With a variety of leadership styles in a team, there is also the possibility that youth will suddenly discover they are being taught in the way they prefer to learn and stop causing trouble. In some cases, however, you may have to deal directly with behavioral problems that threaten to disrupt the group. If you have to mete out discipline, do so in a calm and loving manner. Talk one on one with the youth and/or with their parents. See if you can identify a cause for the problem and ways to deal with it. Ultimately you may have to take serious disciplinary steps so that the group will not be destroyed by one or two persons.

What if I have adult leaders who resist my model of confirmation? How do I work with them?

If you and the appropriate committees in the church have talked through the confirmation model so that they understand what you are doing and why, you can enlist their help in talking with any adults who resist. Or talk with the adults who are resisting. What are their objections? They may have insights into confirmation in your congregation that you need to hear. If the problem is simply "We've never done it that way before," see if there is a way you can help them give up leadership with honor, that is, in such a way that you understand one another and agree mutually that this is the best way to resolve the issue.

What if mentor relationships don't gel?

If it is clear early in the confirmation process that relationships simply aren't working, a change in mentors may take care of the problem. There will always be personality or schedule clashes that keep some relationships from working. If you have two mentors working with a small group (a model many churches are going to), the youth can usually relate to one of the adults.

Helping Youth Claim the Name

Earlier, in Chapter 1, we outlined some goals for confirmation, including these:

● To help youth make commitments to become disciples of Jesus Christ.
● To prepare youth to make their first (or an early) affirmation of faith.
● To help youth prepare for a lifetime of discipleship.

Now you are at the end of the confirmation process. It is time for youth to make decisions about commitments, affirmations, and lifetime discipleship. How do we help them make those decisions?

Decisions, Decisions

At some point, you will have to deal with the reality of prior expectations. Parents expect that their son or daughter will be confirmed. The congregation expects that there will be some "fruit" from the time and effort that goes into the class. You have your own expectations. You work hard with these youth and you would like to have the joy and privilege of confirming them. Youth have expectations of one another. There is an unspoken (sometimes spoken) expectation that everyone will be confirmed, and no one wants to be the "odd one out." These expectations will color the decision-making. There is no way to avoid that reality; but if you are aware of the expectations, they may be less of a problem than if you aren't aware of them.

Regardless of content, nearly all decision-making goes through the same process. It is important to think about alternatives, weigh options, identify and make judgments about consequences, and decide what value we put on which option. As a leader of youth in confirmation, part of your responsibility will be to help youth identify alternative choices, consider consequences, ask the right questions, and develop thoughtful and responsible answers. Then it will be time for you to step out of the picture and let the youth make their own decisions.

> **Part of your responsibility will be to help youth identify alternative choices, consider consequences, ask the right questions, and develop thoughtful and responsible answers. Then it will be time for you to step out of the picture and let the youth make their own decisions.**

What you are asking youth to decide is, Am I willing to make a commitment to Christ and the church? Decisions like this need to be appropriate for the age group. We do not (or at least should not) expect young adolescents to make the kind of mature decision we would expect from an adult. Instead, we help youth see that the decision they make is for where they are today. Tomorrow, or next week, or next year, or years from now, their situation will be different. They will be older, will have had more experience with life, will have raised more questions, and will need to make a commitment that is appropriate for them then.

One of the built-in blessings of a multilevel confirmation approach is that you can say to young adolescents:

"When you are ready to leave high school, we will have in place for you another opportunity. Then you can explore your faith on a different level, more appropriate for that age. At that time you will want to make a new commitment, based on an experience of faith different from the one you have today. But the faith you have today is important. It is where you are right now. So, when you decide to make a commitment, remember it is one that will change as you grow and change. When you answer the questions, your answer will mean, 'Yes, as I understand and experience that now, to the very best of my ability, for today.'"

Such a statement gives youth permission to make faith decisions that are realistic, knowing that their situations will change and so will their commitments.

We also *have* to give youth the freedom to choose. This means we have to set them free to say no. When the confirmation program begins, state clearly that final decisions won't be made until the end and, at that time, each person is free to say yes or no to affirming one's faith and committing to a life of discipleship.

If you use mentors, and if they develop a close working relationship with youth, invite them to talk with the youth about the decision. In a relationship of trust, youth may feel freer to express doubts, raise questions, and in general be more objective than they would with "The Pastor" or in a larger group.

Another possibility: Ask the youth to write a letter describing their decision and the reasons for their choice. Encourage them to be honest and open. Also, ask them to raise questions they'd like to discuss in an interview. These letters should be sent to the pastor or whoever takes primary responsibility for confirmation education. Then the pastor (or whoever is designated) follows up with a personal interview with each youth. In the interview, questions can be explored together, the decision affirmed, and youth and adult can pray together. One advantage of this approach for the pastor is that, if a youth decides not to be confirmed, the pastor can deal with personal feelings about that decision before the interview. Trying to be objective and helpful with a struggling youth is tough when we are feeling disappointed or rejected.

Some congregations hold a retreat to conclude confirmation preparation. The retreat provides time for personal reflection and decision-making. During the retreat, the leadership team tell their own faith stories. One congregation uses older youth for mentors, and their faith stories make a powerful impact on the confirmands. The confirmand/mentor pair (or group) then goes apart to reflect on their confirmation experience, what it has meant to them, and what it means to their future. They describe how God makes a difference in their lives and how they will live out that difference. Closing worship provides a time for affirming decisions.

But What If They Say No?

This is the risk we take when we invite youth to make decisions based on their own experience. They may decide to choose something different from what we had hoped. We have to be willing to run that risk. If we don't, then there is no freedom for the youth involved.

When I was a young preacher, I had a seventh grader say to me, "I don't want to be confirmed. I don't think I'm ready. I want to wait a year, take the class again, and then decide." This was a small town, and everyone knew who was in the confirmation class. I said, "OK, and I'll help you with your parents." Sure enough, he needed help. His parents were upset and angry. What would people think, knowing that their son was the only one in the class not to "join the church"? I tried to say that they might think he was mature enough to know that he wasn't ready, but that was not an answer the parents were eager to hear. Finally, we won the parents' support; and the young man waited a year. The next year he came back to the confirmation class, had a wonderful experience, was confirmed, and is still a loyal disciple of Jesus Christ. If a youth who previously said no to being confirmed doesn't volunteer for this sort of follow-up, it is entirely appropriate for the pastor, mentor, or parents to ask if he or she wants to consider confirmation at this time.

Here are the issues you have to address if a youth says no:

● **Parents.** If you have said from the beginning that the decision is a free one that each youth will make at the end of the process, parents will be more open than if they have been allowed to expect that the decision is only a formality. You will need to spend time reassuring these parents that a "No" decision is actually a sign of maturity rather than a sign of failure. You will need to support the youth against any pressure that might come from parents.
● **Pressure from peers.** There is a common expectation that everyone in the process will be confirmed. Remember that young adolescence is a time when "belonging" is very important, and it takes real courage to stand out against the common expectation. Explain to the whole group that they each made a decision. One or more persons decided not to be confirmed. Remind the youth that they were all free to make a choice and that the church respects and affirms all their choices.

For the most part, however, all the youth in the confirmation process are going to choose to be confirmed. You can give thanks to God for the fruits of your labors and truly celebrate the rite of confirmation.

Confirmation! Rite and Celebrations

How do we conclude the first stage of the confirmation process? How do we celebrate and affirm and ritualize what happened in the process without making it seem like graduation?

Years ago, when I was a first-year student at Garrett (now Garrett-Evangelical Theological Seminary), Dr. Carroll Wise told us a story about his son and the son of a friend. The four of them were on a camping trip. The two boys had just been confirmed and had just been initiated into DeMolay, a youth organization related to the Masonic Order. They didn't remember anything at all about their confirmation—but could recall in vivid detail their DeMolay initiation. In that moment, I decided this would never be the case with youth in my confirmation classes. The role of liturgy and celebration has always been important. Liturgy, when done well, engages all the senses. It appeals to the imagination as well as to the thought processes. We owe it to our youth to make the rite of confirmation as powerful as possible.

> **Liturgy, when done well, engages all the senses. It appeals to the imagination as well as to the intellect. We owe it to our youth to make the rite of confirmation as powerful as possible.**

Begin with the basic liturgy. Baptismal Covenant I (*The United Methodist Hymnal*, pages 33–39) is the foundation for the service of confirmation. Build the service around it. The Baptismal Covenant can easily be adapted to become the order of worship for confirmation Sunday. Use the "Introduction to the Service" as a call to worship. Continue with

- a hymn, preferably one that makes a strong statement about the faith of the church;
- the reading of Scripture;
- prayers;
- a hymn;
- the sermon;
- the response to the word;
- the offertory;
- the acts of baptism and confirmation.

At this point, return to Baptismal Covenant I, beginning with the "Renunciation of Sin and Profession of Faith" (page 34). Do not omit any part of the service, unless there are no youth to be baptized. In that case, you may omit the "Thanksgiving Over the Water." If there are baptisms, be sure to include the entire service.

Every word is carefully chosen to affirm the faith of the church, so it is important that we not omit any of the "Affirmation of Faith" (page 35) or the "Thanksgiving Over the Water." Neither one takes more than forty-five seconds, so "saving time" is not an issue. Every moment of the service should be a time of dignity and power. Attention should be focused on God and God's saving acts, including those acts now taking place in this service of worship.

FAQS About Liturgy, Ritual, and Schedules

We have two services; youth in the confirmation class can be found in both. What do we do about the confirmation service?

One option is to confirm at both services, so that the whole congregation is able to participate in the power of confirmation. Another possibility would be to have the service of confirmation at the early service one year, and the late service the next. Or, if possible, combine the two services for this one Sunday. Make the point that confirmation is one of the most important events of the year, and it is crucial that the entire church be included, whichever approach you choose. The important thing is that you confirm in the midst of the congregation. Confirmation is an act of God and of the whole people of God, and we affirm that reality by the way we schedule the service.

Because we have a tight schedule for worship and a large class, we hold the service of confirmation on Sunday afternoon for parents and families. Is this a good idea?

No. Confirmation is an act of God and of the whole people of God. We downplay that reality and we deny the participation of the congregation by confirming at a time different from the morning worship. Sometimes, however, realities dictate that we have to make choices that are not absolutely theologically consistent. In that case be sure to include mentors, the lay leadership of the church, and others to represent the congregation. But make every effort to confirm in the body of the congregation in the worship service.

Is it really important to include everything in the service of the baptismal covenant? We don't make a big splash when we confirm adults. We just call them up at the end of the worship service and ask them the basic questions.

First, maybe we *should* make a "big splash" when we confirm adults.

Second, particularly with young adolescents, we are praying for a commitment to discipleship through the life of the church. Younger youth are in a "belonging" style of faith. Rites of initiation that make a visual and emotional impact can add to the power of belonging. I've been to Eagle Scout Courts of Honor and initiations into other youth organizations, and I can testify to the power of ritual and symbol in those secular settings. If we want to appeal to youth in a powerful way, we dare not neglect that power in our own rituals.

On a practical and theological note, what would you omit? The "Thanksgiving Over the Water" rehearses God's saving acts in history and invokes the presence of the Holy Spirit. The "Affirmation of Faith" reminds the whole congregation of the faith into which they were baptized, that is, the faith of the church. How could we omit either one of those?

Ways to Make the Service Special

A highly unscientific survey of how United Methodist churches make confirmation a special event reveals some consistency in practice and some very creative ideas. What follows is a compilation of ideas from the survey:

Involve Parents

All the churches responding to the survey involve the parents in the service of confirmation. In all cases, parents (and sometimes siblings) stand behind (or next to) the youth being confirmed and participate in the laying on of hands. Some congregations invite parents to say a "good word" about their youth and/or to offer a blessing to them. As one youth leader said, "The youth are embarrassed by this, but they are embarrassed in a wonderful way. What youth wouldn't remember such a thing?" If you do this, be sure to offer guidance or training to the parents, and be sure they are willing to participate.

Involve the Mentors

As more churches use mentors in the confirmation program, mentors are being included in the service itself. In some churches, the mentor stands up as his or her youth is confirmed. In other churches, mentors participate in the laying on of hands. Several churches indicate that the mentors introduce youth to the congregation by saying "good words" about them and about their growth in faith.

Banners

A growing tradition is the making of special banners for confirmation. (See page 115 in this book for one specific example.)

For churches using *Claim the Name: Confirmation Teaching Plans for 6–15 Weeks*, this resource gives specific help for creating a banner. Each session has a banner symbol as a reminder of the learnings. Patterns are included.

Other congregations have each confirmand create an individual banner that shows who he or she is—interests, feelings, faith, and so on. These banners are hung in the sanctuary for confirmation Sunday and remain there for several weeks.

Gifts

Almost every responding church offers gifts to youth being confirmed. In one church, it is a handcrafted wooden cross made by a congregation member. Another church selects the gifts (so that all are alike); the parents pay for them and present them as a part of the service. The most popular gift from churches is a Bible. However, since many youth receive Bibles in third or fourth grade, some churches give copies of *The United Methodist Hymnal* to youth as they are confirmed.

One congregation takes color pictures of the class and prints them on the front page of their local church's edition of *The United Methodist Reporter*. They also have a "fall-out sheet" with individual pictures of the youth. They place the individual pictures in pewter confirmation frames as a special gift to the confirmands and their families. If your church communication system is less elaborate than this, you can still include names and families of confirmands in the newsletter. Since confirmation is a kind of "birth-day," some churches give candles to youth to be lighted each year on the anniversary of their confirmation.

Meals

A confirmation meal is a big thing in many congregations. Sometimes a breakfast is held on Saturday morning, followed by a rehearsal for the service. Other churches hold a banquet for confirmands, family members, and mentors. One congregation has a catered dinner, but asks the previous year's confirmation class members to decorate the fellowship hall, provide homemade desserts, and act as servers for the meal.

> The danger we run in all the celebration is perpetuating the idea that confirmation is graduation. For most of us, however, the benefits of creating a special day for youth outweigh this danger.

In addition to celebration, the meals often serve as a vehicle for continuing the journey. Some churches include presentations about the youth ministry of the congregation, opportunities for service and mission, and options for growing in the spiritual disciplines.

Other Stuff

In many congregations, the youth and their families leave during the closing hymn to form a receiving line on the church lawn or in the fellowship hall so that the entire congregation can greet them easily. Some churches hold a reception with cake and punch.

Conclusion

So we come full circle. The "birth-day" of the confirmation class reminds us of beginnings. We began confirmation with a vision of young persons claiming the name of Jesus Christ and growing in grace toward sanctification. These youth have now completed a significant part of their journey. It is indeed something to celebrate!

The journey, however, continues. As the youth move forward and grow in faith, find ways to walk with them. They will benefit from your guidance and support. They—and you—will continue to "press on toward the goal for the prize of the heavenly call of God in Christ Jesus" (Philippians 3:14). To God be all honor, glory, and praise!

Selected Bibliography

Adair, Sharon. *Big Differences: How to Deal With Youth of Various Ages*. Nashville: Abingdon Press, 1998.

Baptism Confirmation . . . Implications for the Younger Generation. New York: Department of Youth Ministry, National Council of Churches, USA, n.d.

Baptism, Eucharist, and Ministry. Faith and Order Paper No. 111. Geneva: World Council of Churches, 1982.

Benson, Peter L., and Carolyn H. Eklin. *Effective Christian Education: A National Study of Protestant Congregations*. Minneapolis: Search Institute, 1990.

Benson, Peter L., and Eugene C. Roehlkepartain. *Beyond Leaf Raking*. Nashville: Abingdon Press, 1993.

Browning, Robert L. and Roy A. Reed. *Models of Confirmation and Baptismal Affirmation*. Birmingham, AL: Religious Education Press, 1995.

Browning, Robert L., and Roy A. Reed. *The Sacraments in Religious Education and Liturgy*. Birmingham, AL: Religious Education Press, 1985.

By Water and the Spirit: A Study of Baptism for United Methodists. [study guide by Dwight Vogel] Nashville: Cokesbury, 1993.

By Water and the Spirit: Making Connections for Identity and Ministry. [study guide by Gayle C. Felton] Nashville: Discipleship Resources, 1997.

Dix, Gregory. *The Treatise on the Apostolic Tradition of St. Hippolytus of Rome*. London: SPCK, 1968.

Everson, Thomas J. *Pathways: Fostering Spiritual Growth Among At-Risk Youth*. Boys Town, Nebraska: Boys Town Press, 1993.

Felton, Gayle C. *This Gift of Water: The Practice and Theology of Baptism Among Methodists in America*. Nashville: Abingdon Press, 1992.

Gooch, John O. "Confirmation as Spiritual Formation." *Christians in Education*, Vol. 2, No. 1 (Winter 1995–1996), pp. 7–8.

Gooch, John O. "Some Thoughts Toward a Theology of Confirmation." *Quarterly Review*, Spring 1996, pp. 79–94.

McKinnon, Greg. *The Bottom Line: How to Help Youth Become Disciples*. Nashville: Abingdon Press, 1998.

Roehlkepartain, Eugene C. *The Teaching Church*. Nashville: Abingdon Press, 1993.

Stookey, Laurence Hull. *Baptism: Christ's Act in the Church*. Nashville: Abingdon Press, 1982.

Tertullian. "On Baptism," Volume III in *The Ante-Nicene Fathers*.

Wesley, John. "Treatise on Baptism," *The Works of John Wesley*, 3rd Edition, Volume X. Grand Rapids: Baker Book House.

Westerhoff, John H. *Will Our Children Have Faith?* New York: The Seabury Press, 1976.

For Further Reading

Benedict, Daniel T., Jr. *Baptism and Our Ministry of Welcoming Seekers and Making Disciples*. Nashville: Discipleship Resources, 1996.

Driver, Tom F. *The Magic of Ritual: Our Need for Liberating Rites That Transform Our Lives and Our Communities*. San Francisco: Harper, 1991.

Freire, Paulo. *Pedagogy of the Oppressed: 20th Anniversary Edition*. New York: Continuum, 1993.

Groome, Thomas H. *Christian Religious Education: Sharing Our Story and Vision*. San Francisco, Jossey-Bass, Inc., 1999.

Hill, Paul. *Coming Of Age*. Chicago: African American Images, 1992.

Johnson, Susanne. *Christian Spiritual Formation in the Church and Classroom*. Nashville: Abingdon Press, 1989.

Marty, Martin E. "Rites of Passage I," *The Christian Century*, July 5–12, 1989, page 671.

Prothrow-Stith, Deborah. "Violence Prevention Curriculum for Adolescents." Newton, MA: Educational Development Center, 1987.

Van Gennep, Arnold. *Rites of Passage*. Translated by Vizedon, Monika B. and Caffee, Gabrielle L. Chicago: University of Chicago Press, 1961.

Westerhoff, John H., III. "Confirmation: An Episcopal Church Perspective." *Confirming the Faith of Adolescents: An Alternative Future for Confirmation*. Edited by Arthur J. Lubick. Mahway, NJ: Paulist Press, 1991.